Opening Up to Grief

A Surviving Sibling's Journey with Loss & Love

Janice Jernigan

Green Heart Living Press

Opening Up to Grief:
A Surviving Sibling's Journey with Loss & Love

Copyright © 2022 Janice Jernigan

ISBN Paperback: 978-1-954493-21-6
Cover artwork: Holly Eroh
Cover design: Elizabeth B. Hill

Dedication

To Julie, my loving sister

and those who feel forgotten

Contents

Dear Reader

Your loss is real.

No matter how old you were at the time,
or how long ago it happened.

You deserve to grieve.

Grieving well is the greatest gift you can give yourself.

And, those you hold dear.

Introduction

Do *you* have any siblings?

If you grew up getting a lump in your throat whenever you were the target of this common, seemingly easy-to-answer question, I see you.

For those who have earned the title of 'surviving sibling' before adulthood, I am here with you.

The topic of being a young survivor of sibling loss is rarely thought about, spoken about, or otherwise acknowledged. Siblings of any age, as well as children under five who lose a loved one, are considered 'forgotten mourners' - a description felt by many to be painfully true.

Our loss is often overlooked or deemed less impactful than what others are experiencing.

Everyone needs to be seen and understood. If this basic, human need is not met, it can leave us feeling disoriented and isolated.

When our grief tries to bubble up, in its myriad ways, it feels like there is something wrong with us.

We deserve more than this. We deserve for our loss to be validated. Without this, we are unable to fully and openly grieve.

There is hope. There is another way. How we grieve, and what we are open to receiving, can evolve and expand along with us.

When my sister died, it was a huge loss for me. One that nearly cost me my life. More than once. And, one that will impact the rest of my days. I believe we go through things so we can help others.

While every loss is unique, we can learn and heal from each other's stories. Through sharing my story, I hope it helps you to feel seen and acknowledged for your loss, gain insight into your personal story, and spark a level of healing that is truly transformative.

The personal stories contained within these pages may stir up heavy emotions and long-hidden memories from your own life. Pause when you feel your heart tugging at you. Honor your own story. Make space for your own feelings.

I recommend having a trusted friend, who can hold space for you. Someone who will gently listen to what awakens within you.

If you find you need more structured support, I encourage you to reach out to a grief coach or mental health professional. From personal experience, I can tell you they can help to make the grieving process more manageable.

For those who are a parent, relative, friend, neighbor, teacher, community member, mental health professional - anyone who has influence in the life of a child or adolescent who is a surviving sibling - thank you for being here for us.

My hope is for us to collectively redefine how surviving siblings are viewed, so we can *all* get the help and support we need.

I invite you to join me on this journey.

Part One
Beginnings

My Sister & Me

Julie, my older sister and only sibling, showered me with affection from the moment I arrived. Every chance she got, she held me in her lap, wrapped her arms around me, and hugged me as tightly as she could.

She was my comforter and cheerleader, the person my young eyes fixated on, and the one I most wanted to emulate.

During a summer vacation to the beach, my parents decided to let me sleep in bed with Julie, rather than renting a crib. My sister was five and I was two, so we loved the idea and had a great time bouncing on the bed together.

When we returned home, Julie and I went beyond simply sleeping in the same bed, and crawled into a child-sized sleeping bag together.

We were, quite possibly, the snuggliest of sisters.

We spent our days and nights by each other's side. We were inseparable. My sister was the center of my whole, little universe.

Julie loved me, and I loved her.

In the midst of our second Christmas season together, my five-year-old sister was diagnosed with leukemia - a cancer of blood cells where abnormal cells are produced in the bone marrow. At the time, in the early 1970s, there were treatments for the disease with the goal of inducing remission, yet there was no cure.

The next year and a half were full of ups and downs, which included short remissions followed by agonizing pain, numerous doctor visits before and after a family beach vacation, painful treatments bookending the joint parties for our March birthdays.

Even though Julie was ill during much of our time together, she nurtured me, as big sisters often do.

Two months after celebrating our birthdays, she died. Julie was seven, and I was three years old.

Suddenly, I became a toddler with sad, blue eyes who deeply longed for her sister.

A sister who was not coming back.

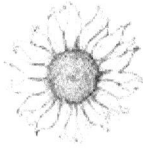

I can only imagine what must have been going through my three-year-old brain. One that, based on what is common for preschoolers, likely did not grasp the concept of permanence.

Why is she no longer eating with my mommy, daddy, and me?

When will she play with me again?

Where does she sleep now?

Did I do something to make her go away?

Will I be okay?

Earliest
Memories

I was standing at the foot of the bed in my parents' bedroom, on the front side of our small brick ranch house. My mom was sitting on the right side of the bed, sobbing profusely. My dad was standing beside her, with one of his arms outstretched rubbing her shoulder, trying to comfort her.

There was an empty hospital bed to the right of their bed, in front of the windows where the sun was shining in. It was bent upward from the middle, so the head of the bed was lifted higher than the rest.

My parents were obviously struck by something that brought deep sadness. I do not know if they saw me there.

I started crying. I did not know why, except that it was what my mom was doing. Crying seemed to fit the mood of the room.

Fast-forward to another scene, an unspecified period of time later...

My parents and I were strolling through an indoor mall. We were at a spot where we could see far into the distance, which revealed a wide-open space with lots of people. My dad broke down into tears. It was an overwhelming cry; one requiring his full attention. We stopped walking, in midstream, so he could compose himself.

I wondered what was the matter. It was not like him to cry. For that matter, it was unusual for me to see either one of my parents crying.

Soon after, the summer after my sister died, my parents and I went to Florida for a short vacation. While it was the same beach and the same time of year we had always gone before, it was not the same.

I missed having Julie by my side and did not like sitting all by myself in the back seat for the long drive. Luckily, my parents needed me close to them, so I made my way to the front seat where my mom held me, tightly, in her lap.

On the trip home, we were stopped at a red light, behind two other cars, when a Cadillac rammed into the back of our car. My mom hit her chin on the top of my head and cracked a couple of her teeth.

While that was the extent of our bodily injuries from the wreck, our car was another story. It was totaled. We were out of town and far from home.

My parents had differing opinions about the meaning of the smoke billowing out of the car. My mom was worried my dad was putting himself in danger by getting too close to it. And, my dad was just as confident he would be okay. He was able to bandage the car up enough for us to make it home safely.

Even though I was a quiet child, I was quick to tell people at church about the car crash. I kept saying, "a catalog hit the back of our car!"

I felt a bit guilty. My mom had two cracked teeth because of me.

These are my earliest memories. Ever. Of anyone, anywhere, or anything. I kept these to myself, for decades, before bringing them up in conversations with my parents.

Through their openness and recollection, I learned the first memory cemented into my consciousness occurred within hours of my sister's death.

My parents had known the end of her short life was near and wanted Julie to be comfortable at home. My paternal grandmother had made arrangements for the hospital bed to be set up in their room. She ensured it was removed almost immediately after my sister died.

My mom and dad were both surprised I recalled the hospital bed. They had never told me about it and did not remember this scene in their room.

Until I brought it up, my memory from the mall had slipped my parents' consciousness. They shared their vague remembrance of a fundraiser for childhood cancer being held across town shortly after Julie died.

In recalling the car crash, my dad said the Cadillac hit our light blue Buick, causing a chain reaction from our car to the two cars in front of us. The forceful impact smashed the trunk of our car, crinkled all four of the side doors, and broke our bench-style front seat in two. The car barely made the trip home and was completely inoperable the next day. Nothing from the car could be salvaged, even for parts.

It gives me chills to consider what may have happened if I had been sitting in the back seat.

In each scene, within my trio of early memories, I can only imagine the intensity of grief being experienced, above and below the surface, by our painfully created family of three.

Last Call

During the last month-and-a-half of Julie's life, my parents had to take her to the doctor almost every day. She was given multiple platelet transfusions in an effort to get her body to go into remission.

My sister was at a point where she could hardly walk. Due to all the injections and blood tests, the bruising on her arms made it hard for the nurses to find a place to draw her blood.

One week before Julie died, her doctor delivered grueling news to my parents: "I believe we are approaching an end."

He did not see how she could last any longer than three weeks.

The doctor assured them nothing more could be done for her in the hospital and was certain she would receive more love and attention at home.

My parents explained to my sister about the doctor saying he could put her in the hospital and she decided she would rather stay at home.

They did not tell Julie she would soon die, yet they believed she knew. On numerous occasions, while screaming with pain, she cried out, "I feel like I'm going to die."

My mom recalls me standing, looking at her as if I was trying to figure it all out. When my big sister needed anything, I desperately wanted to help. Julie would always reply, 'Thank you, baby."

She asked for a hospital bed, so she could be more comfortable. Up until this time, Julie and I had been sleeping in the same bed. Suddenly, my sister and my parents were spending their nights in the same room, while I was alone across the hall.

Over the next several days, we frequently had a house full of company. At times, she enjoyed having visitors. Other times, she asked my parents to make everyone leave the room. Julie was unable to get out of bed, needed more and more pain medications, and wanted to rest.

Friends and family sent cards, books, toys, and a big furry white bear, who promptly became my sister's beloved, stuffed pal.

Julie was in so much pain the doctor told my parents to focus on keeping her comfortable, and not to concern themselves with how many times they gave her pain medication. She slept most of the day. As soon as she woke up, her pain returned. My parents gave her more medicine, and she went back to sleep.

On one particular day, my grandmother came over to spend the night. She stayed in the bedroom with me.

My parents were up with Julie throughout the evening and into the wee hours of the morning. After slivers of sleep for a string of nights, my parents finally fell asleep from pure exhaustion.

My grandmother heard Julie talking deliriously all night long. She could not understand anything my sister said, except she distinctly heard her calling my name. Over and over.

"Janice!… Janice!… Janice!"

A little after six o'clock in the morning, my sister woke up my parents needing to go to the bathroom. My dad helped her sit up in bed, and my mom worked her legs around and off the side of the bed.

Julie did not say anything else. She sat there, in my dad's arms, and took her last breath.

Even as an adult, I can not fully fathom what it was like for my parents to get the doctor's difficult prediction regarding the lifespan of their oldest daughter. And, to experience his words becoming a painful reality. The feeling of helplessness must have been overwhelming.

I am immensely grateful my grandmother was there that night and heard my sister's cries for me. My parents had been too physically and emotionally depleted to hear her and I have no conscious recollection of this.

My sister, this almost surreal character in my life, not only knew my name, she chose to call out for me again and again. Even when her seven-year-old body had very little breath left.

I believe my sister wanted to say goodbye to me. She did, in her own special way.

A Broken Record

A hearse arrived in our driveway a mere fifteen minutes after my dad called the funeral home. Intuitively, my grandmother realized it would not be good for my mom to see Julie's lifeless body being carried out of their room. The two of them went into my bedroom and closed the door.

Before traveling the twenty-minute drive to the cemetery to pay for my sister's grave to be opened, my parents knew they needed to offer me an explanation of what had happened.

How do you bring understanding to a situation you, personally, can not grasp?

Why did my parents lose such a precious child?

Why was her life cut so short?

Why would I be denied the opportunity to grow up sharing my life with my sister?

My parents told me Julie would not be with us anymore. She had gone to heaven to be with Jesus, and would not hurt anymore.

They knew, at three years old, I did not fully comprehend all of what they were telling me. It was as if I thought Julie was just off somewhere and would be coming home at any time.

My parents could tell I had sensed a great loss. Sadness and puzzlement showed in my face, even though I was unable to articulate my feelings.

For several months, I kept telling my mom and dad, "Julie's not going to hurt anymore." I repeated it over and over. "Julie's not going to hurt anymore."

Like a broken record, all of what I knew had been irrevocably scratched. I was innately aiming to make sense of a senseless situation, while at the same time, bringing comfort to my parents and to myself.

"Julie's not going to hurt anymore." Each time they heard me say this, they assured me I was right.

Julie's *not* going to hurt anymore. The same could not be said for those she left behind.

It is beyond my comprehension how, in the immediate aftermath of losing their oldest daughter, my parents summoned the strength to deliver this monumental news to three-year-old me.

How do you describe death to the little sister left behind, when they have no concept of its finality?

How do you let your preschooler know their closest human, playmate, and best friend is gone forever?

How do you explain to a toddler that life, as they knew it, would never, ever be the same?

I wonder how a three-year-old senses a broken heart. The ones belonging to my parents, grandparents, and everyone else whom my sister had touched.

I wonder how disorienting it was for my toddler-sized body to become the only inhabitant of the double bed I had shared with Julie.

I wonder how I felt my own enormous loss. A loss that would completely disrupt and permanently change my life.

Part Two
Beyond Tears

Into the Closet

During my post-Julie preschool years, I spent time in the closet. My bedroom, the one I previously shared with my sister, had a long, narrow closet along one wall, with two sliding wooden doors.

It was the perfect size for me to fit on the floor inside the right-side door, along with my two large, stuffed animal friends.

Winnie the Pooh was about two feet tall and almost as wide. He had short, yet permanently open, arms and legs. Along with his red, stitched-on smile, he looked as if he were ready to embrace me at any moment.

My other companion was a big, furry white bear, who had been Julie's beloved pal in her final days. He was a bit more reserved and seemed to have a quiet knowing. While he had surely seen a lot of suffering and sadness, he was strong enough to stick around to be with me.

I purposefully gathered the two of them and headed to the closet, where I closed the door and sat in the dark.

It was a calm and nurturing space for me. A place I did not share with anyone else. It was a tiny corner in my little world where I could soothe myself.

Whenever the time was interrupted by one of my parents, I felt like I had been caught. And, I was right.

I was caught grieving in my own way.

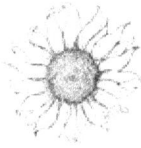

Outside the closet, when I played with my other stuffed animals and dolls, Winnie the Pooh and the big, furry white bear generally stayed in the background.

Looking back, I realize, they were my comforter and confidante. Their primary role was to serve as my grief buddies, and I am grateful for each one of them.

As I grew in both age and height, I regularly laid on my bedroom floor with the top part of my body inside the right side of my closet, and the rest of me sprawled out into the room.

It evolved into a nook where I quietly colored the pages of a coloring book. As I became more and more active in the space, Winnie the Pooh and Julie's beloved, furry pal joined me less and less.

I had created my own, personal sanctuary.

Our First Grade Teacher

Julie was worried she might not be promoted to second grade. She had only been half-finished with a test when she started feeling ill. It was one of the many times my mom needed to pick her up early from class.

When my sister was unable to return to school, the teacher encouraged her classmates to create cards filled with well-wishes. Mrs. Fuller, her kind and thoughtful teacher, personally delivered the hand-crafted artwork, along with her schoolwork, to Julie at our house. She also brought her report card.

My sister made all A's for the fourth quarter of the school year. On her scholastic achievement test, she scored equivalent to a sixth-grader in spelling and a fourth-grader in math.

This really meant a lot to Julie. She had achieved her goal of being promoted to second grade.

Four years later, Mrs. Fuller became my first-grade teacher. I had a much different experience with her. She assigned a long list of homework, which felt overwhelming to me.

On more than one occasion, I was given a pink slip of paper to take home for my parents to sign. This required an admission that I had fallen short of what was expected of me. It felt like something beyond what I could allow to happen.

As soon as I got home, I made a beeline to my parents' bathroom and flushed the evidence of my shortcomings down the toilet. I never heard a word about it from anyone - my parents, my teacher, no one. It was as if it had truly disappeared.

My other, harsher memory of Mrs. Fuller is when, for the first time in my life, I got scolded for talking during class. As a super quiet child, I was surprised the teacher thought it was me.

Mrs. Fuller took me out of the classroom and walked me down the hall. Without a word, she escorted me to a small room and shut the door behind us. She told me I was about to get a spanking.

She then left me alone in the room. I did not know what I had done to deserve it. I could not point to a specific action on my part that led to this impending result. Oddly enough, no one else was being punished in this way.

After what felt like forever to a child with little concept of time, the teacher returned with a wooden paddle. This was especially scary. My parents had never used a paddle when I got in trouble at home. Even more so, they had talked of other parents using belts or paddles to whip their children and felt it was unnecessary.

With only her and I in the room, Mrs. Fuller spanked me with the paddle several times. While doing so, she asked me if I was sorry. For what? I did not know, and it did not seem like an appropriate time to ask. It was as if she was waiting for me to shed tears to show remorse for whatever wrongdoing I had committed. Once I acted like I was crying, she stopped.

From a physical perspective, getting paddled was not painful. Emotionally, it crushed my spirit.

I was humiliated and ashamed.

I was determined not to let my parents, or anyone else, find out. Mrs. Fuller was not just *any* teacher, she was Julie's *highly praised* teacher. The one my mom regularly talked about as being a wonderful person.

Perhaps, she knew something about me I did not yet know. I must have deserved to be reprimanded in such a way.

When recounting the teacher's visit to our house during Julie's final days, my mom shared: "I know it was very hard for Mrs. Fuller to see her like that. I could tell she was fighting back the tears, and so was I."

I wonder what it was like for the teacher to lose a young, promising student.

I wonder how it impacted her as a person, as well as her teaching style.

I wonder how I might have stirred up painful memories of my sister for her.

In first grade, I learned how to write my name and other common words. I also obtained insights, beyond the stated curriculum, and experienced many firsts.

The first time I felt a deep sense of shame. The first time I was unfairly punished. The first time I thought something was wrong with me. The first time I felt singled out. Different. Less than.

The first time I felt unlovable.

A Child's Fantasy

I did not cherish bedtime. Like many children, I was inventive in finding ways to extend the time my mom or dad spent in my room with me.

One of my favorite tactics was asking for something to drink. I knew neither one of my parents could resist my request.

Usually, one would fetch the water, while the other sat on my bed and talked with me about inconsequential things. Like clockwork, the other parent soon returned with a small, paper cup, filled with water to quench my sudden, bedtime-induced thirst.

I always took my first sip in *slooowww* motion.

Between each sip, I took a deliberate pause to share something about my day. Since this bedtime ritual took place within hours of supper at our kitchen table, I had to get creative about what more I could share about my day's adventures.

When I got closer to the bottom of the cup, with its delicately designed flowers, I took smaller sips and longer breaks between each one.

As I grew older, I made enhancements to this tried-and-true sleep time-postponing tactic: getting the other person talking. Whether it was my mom, dad, or both of them, I learned to tap into my talent for asking dialogue-starting questions. At the time, I had minimal interest in my parents' answers.

My mission was to make going to bed a long, drawn-out process. With nightly practice, I became a child-sized expert for making three ounces of liquid last far beyond my bedtime.

This gave me a sense of control over how long my parents stayed in my presence.

Over time, our bedtime dance evolved. While I had gotten better and better at stalling, my parents were on to me. They sharpened their own tactics: giving me less to drink and prodding me to drink faster. Eventually, they modified the process and made me responsible for getting my own cup and finishing it before going to bed.

Much changed, yet one thing remained the same: my fantasy.

After the nighttime sip-sparring with my parents, my personal pretend-time was in full force. I laid on my back, arms by my side, with my palms facing up.

One-by-one people, without specific faces, came to visit me in my bedridden state. They were concerned about my condition and wanted to check in on me.

No words were spoken. At times, these invisible visitors reached out to hold my hand.

This silent, one-act play without an audience was frequent and long-running, from the time I was a small child and into my teenage years.

It was my biggest fantasy.

A fantasy of being seen.

Before Julie died, I was not aware of the concept of being alone. I had never before known a world without my sister.

In an instant, it became my new reality. The double bed my sister and I once shared became a stark reminder of how my life had changed.

I was swimming in a sea of emptiness and uncharted waters.

My make-believe hospital bed was an element of the days and nights we had shared. It was what I knew, and presented a symbol of importance. A tangible sign that others cared.

I wonder if I was craving the attention Julie had recently received while she was seriously ill.

I wonder what it was like to go from giggling in bed with my older sister to a deafening silence when she was gone.

I wonder if I thought, by mimicking her, I could somehow transport myself to wherever Julie was now sleeping.

I wonder what it was like to abruptly begin spending the long stretch of hours, between my bedtime and wake-up time, alone.

I wonder if I slept much at all.

For many years, I slept with my dolls and stuffed animals all around me, covering the perimeter of the bed. This was partly for company, so I would not be alone, and partly because I did not want any of them to feel like they were unable to join me.

I knew how it felt to be left behind.

I sensed my hospital role-play, with its imaginary characters, was not a good thing to share with anyone.

I thought something was wrong with me for yearning to capture a twinkle of the limelight.

In more recent years, I learned this kind of pretend play is not uncommon in young children who lose a sibling after an extended illness. It is a makeshift method for processing what happened.

Perhaps, it was my personal way of grieving.

Childhood Dream Scene

I was quite a kicker during the night. Sometimes, I kicked so much the sheets came off at least one corner of the bed.

On periodic occasions, when my dad was out of town and I slept with my mom, she awoke with stories of how I had kicked her all night long. Whenever I spent the night at my grandparents' house, my grandmother told similar tales after sharing her bed with me.

Sometimes, I added boxing to the mix with erroneous punches and arm extensions onto my bedmate.

I felt bad about lashing out in my sleep, even though it was not something I could control.

And, I had no memory of it.

When I was a toddler and young girl, I had a recurring dream. I was dressed in beautiful, long, and flowy garments while riding an elephant inside a castle.

Within this scene without a story, it felt as though I had entered into another world. A page torn out of a picture book, with me as its only character.

As I awoke, I was a bit confused about what had just happened. It came across as odd to me. I was not sure how to articulate it, so I kept it to myself.

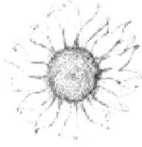

While it is common for preschoolers and young children to move when slumbering, these movements can be amplified by stress, anxiety, and traumatic events. These have been shown to negatively impact sleep and cause fitful, tantrum-like disturbances.

I wonder if my physical being was trying to find Julie in what was now my own bed.

Since children are early in life and have little context for the broader world, it was not unusual for the images visiting me in my sleep to create a single scene, rather than an actual storyline.

When I was a senior in high school, I rode an elephant at the zoo with a close friend of mine. She had a fondness for these massive mammals. In this real-life adventure, I found it a little scary to be up so high. In my dream, I felt secure and full of wonder.

As I grew older, I wanted to explore around the castle, yet always awoke before riding the elephant more than a few steps.

Given the frequency of my recurring dream as a child, and my lingering recollection of it into adulthood, I searched for its meaning.

I found my imagination's choice of clothing to be a dream symbol for a free spirit who tends to not fit into societal norms.

As a child who had lost my only sibling, I was different. I did not know anyone like me.

Riding an elephant, the largest living land animal, is a sign of strength to overcome situations in waking life. It denotes something one will not forget and is connected to a level of helplessness and lack of control, feeling invisible, and the need to take control of one's life.

It took a certain kind of strength to be a surviving sibling and to face all that came with the arrival of this profound life change. There was much I could not control. I did not feel truly seen and had not yet learned the importance of taking ownership of my own life.

The spacious castle I was in, one with curved, gray stone walls, is an indication of the need for private space.

By going into the closet with my stuffed animal friends, I was intuitively on track in meeting my need for alone time.

Kelly Bulkeley, author of *Dreamcatching: Every Parent's Guide to Exploring and Understanding Children's Dreams and Nightmares,* has found, "Dreams are very accurate, in many ways, in recollecting the basic concerns and emotional issues in our lives."

Through reflecting and learning about my childhood dream, I gained insight into my identity, as well as my deepest needs and feelings at the time.

My simple yet vivid dream scene was communicating what my young, conscious mind could not formulate into words.

Family Photos

Growing up, I always knew I had a sister. Even though I do not have any of my own memories of her.

Without being able to recall and verbalize my own memories of Julie, I have been dependent on my parents and other family members to share their memories with me.

It is always through their uniquely personal lens, rather than mine, that I get glimpses of Julie.

There were no family photos framed and on display anywhere in our house.

I did not realize this was outside what was typical until I was old enough to spend afternoons in the homes of friends from church or school. It was the first time I saw a family photo wall. A large swath of vertical space, usually with professionally made and carefully hung, framed photos of the full family and its individual members.

My parents captured quite a few photos of Julie and me during our childhood days together. As was common at the time, the film was developed into two-inch square slides mounted on paperboard.

It was a deliberate action to look at physical images of the sister I had lost. To see them required a slide projector and a blank wall in our house.

My first recollection of viewing the slides is from when I was around ten years old. It was unlike anything I had ever experienced: the hum of the small motor in the projector, the heat emitting from the lamp, and the dust particles flashing like mini stars as they floated in the air in front of the large white square on the wall.

Almost like magic, the girl who was my sister popped into view.

The slides included Julie as a baby and toddler and progressed into showing the two of us. One of the images showed me standing behind Julie, who was seated on the floor inside the legs of a wooden kitchen chair turned on its side. Her arms were slightly elevated while resting on the horizontal legs of the chair.

I was showcasing what had become known in our family as my signature 'scrunchy faces.' The sound of Julie cackling with laughter could almost be heard through the screen.

A typical viewing session included my dad adjusting the screen, fine-tuning the focus, and advancing the slides, while my mom shared a verbal caption for each scene as it sprung into view from the circular tray. She looked sad, as if she were trying her best to contain something inside. On a few occasions, the emotional dam gave way to a flood of tears. I did not know what to do to ease my mom's pain.

My sister's illness was a backdrop to the story.

Like clockwork, it was offered as context for when we advanced toward the slides where she had gained a great deal of weight, due to the mound of medications she needed to take. As the slides progressed through our life as a family of four, Julie was wearing a highly conspicuous wig to conceal her hair loss from chemotherapy and radiation treatments.

One of my mom's most beloved photos is of Julie and me, sleeping peacefully in our bed beside each other. My mom tells the story of seeing how precious we looked together, so much so, she could not resist capturing the moment. It is the only image showing my sister without hair.

A slew of slides served as visual proof: the two of us were sisters who shared a close bond. We were together much more than we were apart.

We deeply loved each other.

Julie was frozen in time as the happy-go-lucky,

outgoing child who was not afraid of anything, including witnessing to the neighbors, imploring them to be saved so they could go to heaven.

This was one of my mom's favorite stories. It was sparked by the slide depicting my sister, in her swimming cap, running through a yard sprinkler, while playing with our closest neighbors.

It was a story I grew weary of hearing. Being the quiet child left behind, it felt like yet another way my sister was better than me. Better than I would ever be.

As a preteen and teenager, I looked forward to a particular slide. One of my sister by herself, dressed for church, with her freshly-combed long, straight, light brown hair. She was standing on the edge of our carport, leaning over the trunk of our family sedan with one arm outstretched above her, and pouting.

Whenever the image appeared, I tried to keep it on the screen for as long as possible. I accomplished this by asking questions: When was this? What had made Julie unhappy? Why was she pouting? My parents never remembered the answers, which was almost irrelevant.

This was the only evidence my eyes had ever seen that my sister was less than perfect, and was not above having what was considered to be negative emotions.

The picture conveyed the message I was longing to receive: Julie was human.

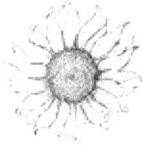

We had a stack of carousels, filled with slides, chronicling our time as a family of four. And yet, there are only two slides, spanning the same few moments, with the four of us pictured together.

The photos were taken at Christmastime, although they did not include any holiday decor. In one photo, we are all sitting on the couch. I am in my dad's lap, and Julie is in my mom's lap.

For the other one, we are all sitting on the floor in front of the couch. None of us has a genuine smile in either photo.

Our family of four never had the experience of posing for corny, yet traditional, professional photos.

Years later, as an adult with many visits to other people's houses, I asked my parents about the absence of family photos on display.

My mom shared the conundrum. It was too painful to see photos of Julie around the house, yet felt as if it would be disrespectful to display pictures of our family without her.

This quandary extended to our lives beyond photos. How do you balance reminiscing about someone who has died, while also embracing the moment we are living?

In many ways, my memories of Julie live in slides. It was one of the few spaces where I could predict, with great certainty, her name would be spoken.

Through the years, I have had mixed feelings about seeing images of my sister and me projected onto a blank wall within our home. It reconnects me to the sister I lost and reignites my longing to recall my own memories of her.

I treasure the photos of Julie and me. The ones showing our genuine interactions, our closeness, and our love for each other.

I also appreciate those showing glimpses of the difficult realities we were facing, and the humanness embedded in each one of us.

Including my sister.

The Power of the Pen

The summer after seventh grade, while on vacation, I met a boy in the hotel pool. My parents were less than thrilled about it. Nevertheless, he and I became pen pals.

I found one of the letters I had written to him, yet never mailed. It read:

"*I don't know why my parents don't like you. I do. I guess they're also just a little overprotective.*

You see, I think I told you that I'm an only child. Well, I am now. I used to have a sister. She was four years older than me. She got this disease called leukemia. She died when I was three years old.

I guess my parents are just scared that they'll lose me. They've already lost one daughter. I know it was hard for them, so I feel sorry for them. I miss my sister, too.

Whenever people talk about how lucky I am to be an only child, I get so mad. I know they don't mean to make me mad because most people don't know about my sister.

Thanks for letting me tell you this, I had to tell someone.

My parents say they understand, but they don't. They have brothers and sisters, I don't."

In eighth grade, my English teacher included writing as a consistent part of the curriculum. Each week, at the beginning of class, she directed us in writing about a specific topic.

One of the early prompts she gave us was: Write about your summer vacation. I wrote about going to the beach, including the boy I met and mentioned him calling me one day while visiting my hometown. I got a check-plus on the assignment, along with a 'what happened?' comment from the teacher.

On a different week, the teacher jump-started our thinking with: Write about a painful experience. The first sentence of my assignment began:

"I haven't really had a painful experience, at least if I have, it wasn't painful enough for me to remember it."

I then proceeded to write about a small cut I had gotten on my finger when pulling on a string in the carpet. I shared that I felt stupid for not realizing it was attached. This earned me a check-plus.

A month later, the teacher gave us the prompt: Write about something you will never forget. This sparked me to write about Julie:

> *"One thing that I will never forget is my sister. I was only three when she died of leukemia, but I'll never forget her.*
>
> *The main thing I remember about her is when some people brought a hospital bed to our house, so she could sleep on it in my parent's room, just in case something happened.*
>
> *Another thing is I remember right after she died, I was with my parents and they were crying, I didn't know what to do, so I cried too. Back then, I didn't know why I was crying, but now I understand.*
>
> *I know what it's like to not have a sister, but I don't know what it's like to be an only child. Even though I don't have any brothers or sisters, I'm not an only child. If I was, I would've never had a sister.*
>
> *Even now, whenever someone talks about their brothers and sisters, I sometimes wish I had a sister.*
>
> *Every time someone talks about how they hate their sisters, I want to tell them, what if they died!"*

The teacher awarded me a check-plus on my paper.

This time, she did not add any comments.

These writings, from my first year as a teenager, offer a glimpse into how losing Julie impacted my new world and personal perspectives.

They provide me with a different level of insight.

Based on my teacher's comment, the boy at the beach was of greater interest than the sister I had lost. I wonder how this reaction was absorbed by thirteen-year-old me.

Part Three
Being Loved

A Surrogate Sisterhood

After Julie died, our pediatrician recommended my parents enroll me in preschool. They heeded his advice, and I attended classes as a three and four-year-old. Since I had become an only child, both at home and at most of our extended family gatherings, this offered me a chance to interact with other children.

Around the time I turned five years old, a girl my age moved into the house two doors up the street from me. I vividly remember this blonde-haired girl sitting at the edge of her yard, with her bare feet on the cement separating the grass from our asphalt neighborhood road. It was an area like a gully where water would rush through on a rainy day or when someone was washing their car. My dad encouraged me to go talk to her. Though I was hesitant to be so outgoing, I did so.

It was the day Tahlia and I first became playmates.

I immediately admired how she could fearlessly run, barefoot, through our large front yards, while I gingerly hopped, carefully and deliberately, from spot to spot on clumps of grass.

She had three half-siblings, all well into their teenage years when we first met. In many ways, my new friend was being raised as if she were an only child. At this point in my life, it felt like something we had in common.

Our closest neighbors, those in the house between Tahlia and me, as well as the ones who lived across the street from me, each had a set of sisters around our age.

As we grew older, we spent many sunny afternoons playing softball in the backyard of our common next-door neighbor. The girl across the street joined us, while her older sister, who was Julie's age, believed she was too old to play with us.

I wonder if this was how she, or her parents, managed the grief of losing her seven-year-old friend a few years earlier.

For our pickup game of ball, we used large trees, conspicuously spaced, to form somewhat of a diamond, for first, second, and third bases. Home base was rarely specified. Inevitably, the two sisters got into an argument, which tended to escalate quickly.

The rest of us quietly dispersed, as if part of a pre-written script. Tahlia and I soon became our own pairing. Our relationship steadily evolved and entered into the realm of 'best friend' designation.

Even though the two of us went to different elementary schools, we spent every moment we could in each other's company. We played together, ate meals together, and - barring school nights - spent the night together at my house. Tahlia went to church with me for the children's activities on Wednesday nights, and we routinely wore each other's clothes.

If you saw one of us, odds were you saw the other.

This became even more true when I switched from a private, Christian school to the public middle school. For the first time in our lives, Tahlia and I went to the same school and rode the bus together in the mornings and afternoons.

We found time, while in separate classes, to write notes to each other. We shared our unfiltered thoughts about whatever was important to us - from who we liked to how bored we were at that moment.

Tahlia and I became highly skilled at folding lined notebook paper into a small rectangle with a triangle-shaped tab for easy opening. We adorned the outer parts with a plethora of abbreviated messages: BFF, best friends forever, W/B/S, write back soon, and FYEO, for your eyes only.

Our favorite acronym, LYLAS, love ya like a sister, could be found on every letter we exchanged.

At the end of sixth grade, when my family moved to the other side of the highway, we started consuming longer stretches of each other's time. On weekends, it was assumed Tahlia would be spending the night with me, and my family began including her in our annual beach vacation.

We knew we would be best friends forever, and fantasized about having each other as the maid of honor in our weddings.

In the summer between seventh and eighth grade, Tahlia and I elevated our best friend status to include dressing alike. We had multiple outfits that were exactly the same.

It was not uncommon for strangers to mistake us for twins, even though Tahlia was a few inches taller than me. This slight height differential caused her to be sent home from school one day, because her shorts were considered too short to meet the dress code. We both stopped wearing those shorts - the ones with the brightly-colored flowers - to school.

People automatically assumed we were sisters.

Sometimes, we let them believe we were. In many ways, we *felt* like sisters. She was the sister I had never had, or so my conscious mind believed, and I welcomed the chance to have a sister in my life.

Even though Tahlia was just under five months younger than me, I held the role of the older sister.

While I was shy and bashful around nearly everyone else, adults and children alike, I was the confident leader of our relationship. When we were growing up, I chose which dolls or barbies would be part of our playtime scenarios.

In our early teens, I was usually the instigator of inviting her to my house, and the decider of what we did during our time together. I was the teacher, and she was my student. I was the dominant one, and we were still the bestest of friends.

Tahlia 'got me' - she understood me like no one else had. No one since Julie. And, by this age, I could not recall or articulate any personal memories of her. Julie seemed more like a character in a storybook than my real-life sister.

When we started high school, the tight bond Tahlia and I shared began showing a few loose threads. We primarily saw each other at school and wrote notes back and forth to each other during our classes. We did not share any of the same classes, and both of us were becoming more interested in spending time with boys.

About the same time, we started making different friends. I could sense Tahlia was getting closer to one particular friend, more so than with me.

She was my best friend. I did not want to lose her.

In what felt like a short period of time, and with greater frequency, our phone conversations ended with one of us mad or upset with the other.

Our rhythmic see-saw of note writing was getting out of balance, and beginning to feel one-sided. Rather than responding to me with a hand-written note, Tahlia made excuses about being too busy in class. I knew in my heart this was not true, yet I wanted to believe it.

Weeks passed, and one day, she appeared to be in a good mood. This had become a rare occurrence when we were together, so I was both surprised and pleased. Tahlia and I walked around the school while we chatted and caught up with each other. She promised to write me a note as we both scurried off, in different directions, to our next class.

I was elated and feeling lucky to have a friendship strong enough to withstand the turbulence we had been experiencing.

Finally, we were getting back on track.

After class, she and I met by the concessions, a place we had arranged earlier. When we came within talking distance, Tahlia handed me a note.

I was ecstatic. This was the first letter she had written to me in recent history.

I tucked the note into one of my books and asked if she wanted to join me as I headed to the locker we shared. She said she was waiting to meet another friend and would join me as soon as she could.

After getting my books from our locker, I could not wait any longer. I hurriedly opened Tahlia's note to me and began reading.

I did not like what she had written. It was a 'Dear Janice' letter terminating our friendship. Along with a list of all the things wrong with me. A compilation of my faults.

I did not know whether to cry or be mad. I wanted to do both. I could not believe she would treat me this way. It shocked me to my core.

Why would my best friend, for the past two-thirds of my life, do something like this?

What happened?

How could she suddenly disappear from my life?

It felt like I was losing a sister all over again. Except this time, I had a decade full of fond memories I could easily recall.

While it was never the same, Tahlia and I became friends again during our junior year. She joined my parents and me on a trip to the beach during spring break.

Over the next couple of years, we had a handful of conversations. She represented comfort for me. I usually reached out when I was down and needed a pick-me-up or wanted to celebrate a recent accomplishment. She typically responded with short words or phrases, uttered almost robotically.

I lacked the interpersonal skills to fully rebuild our relationship, and she seemed to lack the desire. I longed to recreate the closeness we once shared, but it was not to be.

At the time, I did not have the words to fully express my feelings, yet the ache within my heart felt all too familiar.

Adored by a Boy

Throughout my elementary and middle school years, I always had a crush on a boy. At least one. Most of the time, the subject of my infatuation did not like me at nearly the same level if they liked me at all.

Soon after I entered high school, that changed. Early in my freshman year, I met Jed.

We were classmates in English and quickly began to form a friendship. He loved to play Dungeons and Dragons and shared his hobby with me through his intricate drawings of favorite characters. I looked forward to Jed's notes to me between classes, a welcome benefit of our budding friendship.

Before long, we expressed a mutual interest in taking our relationship to the next level: 'going together' as boyfriend-girlfriend. The only place we could actually 'go together' was in the hallways at school. My parents had a rule I could not go on a date with anyone until I turned fifteen.

We compensated by spending hour upon hour chatting with each other on the phone.

When the end-of-year holiday break arrived, our connection was unphased. The generously lengthy, coiled cords attached to our wall-hung telephones gave us the privacy we craved during our daily marathon conversations. We could actively walk, or find a cozy spot to lounge, while we talked about any and everything on our minds.

During a series of these phone calls, I gave Jed a virtual makeover. I guided him through how to upgrade his clothing and get a haircut to bring his overall look to be more on-trend. This immediately boosted his confidence. It felt good to know I had played a role in helping him.

In the New Year, when Jed and I returned to our classroom, he no longer looked like a boy. He had transformed into a guy. A guy I continued to like, and just as important, a guy who still liked me.

Our genuine care for one another had grown by leaps and bounds.

A few months later, we went on our first date. It was my fifteenth birthday. Jed's parents took us out to eat for dinner, before dropping us off at the nearby movie theater. We saw *Mannequin*, a romantic comedy in which a beautiful, window display model springs to life and falls in love.

In the months that followed, Jed and I began spending more time together. He was easy to talk to and we formed a closer and closer bond. Over time, our relationship extended beyond boyfriend-girlfriend status.

We became best friends. A role in my life that had been open since Tahlia decided to vacate it months before.

Jed and I loved each other, as deeply as two fifteen-year-old hearts have the capacity to love.

We talked about getting married one day. We were also practical and wanted to go to college first. When daydreaming about our future, we decided we would marry when we turned twenty-one.

I was counting down the years until we would become husband and wife. It would also be the day his sister, who was two years younger than us, would officially become my sister too.

When I turned sixteen, I could not wait to get my driver's license. Since I was four months older than Jed, getting my license represented our collective independence. It meant we could drive to and from our time together without needing to coordinate a pick-up or drop-off with either one of our parents.

The ink was barely dry on my temporary paper license when I put my newfound freedom into action. I drove to see Jed compete in a karate tournament.

This marked the beginning of the next chapter of our relationship. One in which we could spend seemingly endless blocks of time together.

Stone Mountain Park was a common destination for our excursions. It was less than five miles away from where we each lived, and there were plenty of things to do and explore.

Our favorite spot had a single entry point: a nearly 100-year-old covered bridge with lattice-like sides. When driving across it, in my Chevrolet Chevette hatchback, the clackety-clack of its rickety slats were readily apparent.

It was worth it to reach the park's largest island. Jed and I enjoyed the scenery and seclusion it offered, amid its lightly traveled trails and massively large boulders. We regularly settled in a spot near the lake surrounding the island. It was a peaceful place to immerse ourselves in nature.

We spent almost every free moment together.

Jed joined me for family meals and celebrations with my parents, grandparents, aunt, uncle, and cousin. He came along, with my parents and me, on a beach vacation with carefully orchestrated sleeping arrangements.

He was a willing partner when taking my much younger cousin to the local game ranch, where we all got a rush from feeding the animals.

Jed was a shy guy with a quiet presence. I was his take-charge girlfriend. Since he did not have his own car, I was the literal, and in many ways figurative, driver of our relationship.

When he started having other close friends, both male and female, I did not like it. I saw it as taking time away from us and feared it would ultimately lead to him drifting away from me. This caused arguments between us, and several times, resulted in us breaking up with each other.

Just as I typically initiated the breakup, I was also the one who took the lead in bringing us back together. During one particular parting-ways conversation, I asked if we could remain friends. Without hesitation, Jed firmly and confidently responded with an astonishing, "No."

Our relationship was coming to an abrupt end.

No more option to be friends, which could lead to being more than friends. No more chapters to be written for the two of us.

With this tiny, two-letter word, I was losing the future I fully believed we would spend together. The future I had assumed was safe, secure, and set in stone.

It was becoming a story with a predictable ending. Love until you cannot love anymore, then disappear completely from my life.

This is how my heart remembers the final breakup with my first love. In reality, it was a mutual decision and had a much less dramatic ending.

When asked the pivotal question of remaining friends, Jed said he thought it would be better if we "made a clean break for a while" until we had truly gotten over our break up.

Jed had become the centerpiece of my life.

He told me he was worried about me. Without asking, I knew what he meant.

As much as my heart was breaking, my mind was racing and quickly being overrun by my own set of questions.

Why was I losing someone I loved?

What would I do without my best friend?

How could I possibly move on with my life?

Deep, Dark, Depressing Days

A year earlier, at the beginning of our tenth-grade year, Jed and I remained good friends. We had dated for much of our freshman year.

When I realized I wanted to date him again, I told him how I felt. He did not feel the same way towards me. My first love had moved on and was dating someone else.

Soon after learning this, I wrote a journal-like entry on my typewriter at home:

> *"I was so depressed that I began to believe that my life was no longer worth living. It was then when I started having serious thoughts of just ending it all. It wasn't too long before Jed caught on to what was going on inside of me. He begged me to change my mind, and give my problems some more time.*

He said everything he could think of to convince me that it wouldn't be worth it. Jed even offered to break up with his girlfriend, saying that I meant much more to him than she ever would.

As the days lingered on, he continued telling me how much he cared for me. Jed said that if I ever committed suicide, that he would also, because he couldn't bear to live without me. I assured him that I was aware of how much he cared for me, which led him to ask why I was still planning to kill myself, knowing how much he loved me.

Before I was able to respond, he added that I was being very selfish, thinking of my own problems, not giving thought to all the grief I would bring to the people who care about me.

Jed never gave up, he kept trying to change my mind. He would compare my month of unhappiness to my other years of happiness. It was impossible to outdo his words.

It was not until after a few long weeks of nothing but conversations with Jed about suicide, and reasons not to do it, that I finally changed my mind."

One day, amidst this string of conversations, I had a bottle of over-the-counter medication sitting on the kitchen counter in front of me. I was on the phone with Jed and told him I was about to overdose on pain pills.

Almost immediately, he and his mom came over and got me out of my house. They kept me under their watchful eye all afternoon.

Having suicidal thoughts was not new to me.

I first remember having them when I was in seventh grade. A lot of boys, including some I had a mild crush on, made fun of my last name. They were relentless. I could not get away from their snide, sing-songy ridicules of me, and frequently came home from school deeply upset and in tears.

My parents wanted desperately to help me and were at their wits' end for what to do. I wanted to change my first, middle, and last name. After many conversations, they convinced me to keep the first and middle names they had given me.

Over the summer, my parents filed the paperwork and legally changed my last name.

This resolved the bullying.

I let those who inquired about my name change make up their own story behind the reason why. No one guessed the real reason. I kept it to myself.

Months after Jed and his mom thwarted my attempt at ending my life, he broke up with his girlfriend. The two of us quickly picked up where we had left off in our boyfriend-girlfriend relationship.

I added to my journal:

"If I had ended my life before, I would never have had the chance to feel the happiness I now feel.

Jed and I have been together now for over four months, and we plan to stay together forever. Although I can't say that nothing will ever change our plans, I am very excited about my future.

I feel like I owe Jed a lot for staying by my side through the bad times of my life. Had he not been there, I would probably not be here today."

Jed and I stayed together throughout our sophomore year and for much of the following summer. We made a clean break from each other a few weeks before the start of our junior year.

When he was the first person I saw at school registration, he briefly said hello before walking away. As I jotted down in my journal at the time, *"Afterwards, I felt depressed because seeing him stirred up all those memories I had of us."*

I managed to make it through the first half of my junior year without Jed as my boyfriend. We did not have any classes together, and it was rare for me to see him in the hallways at school.

On the first day of the second half of the school year, things changed. Jed was in one of my classes.

I could not bear the thought of seeing my former boyfriend and best friend each and every day for an uninterrupted period of time. I missed the next few days of school.

My parents found themselves in a difficult situation once again. They wanted to help me, yet were uncertain how to do so. For me, one thing was certain. I was not going back to school. My dad returned my books and completed the paperwork to withdraw me from all of my classes.

I officially became a high school dropout.

Months later, I wrote:

"Towards the middle of my junior year of high school, I felt as though I could not go on any further. It seemed as though the world was against me, and I was left to stand alone. Although I have never considered myself to be a strong person, my weaknesses were really beginning to take over my life.

I wanted so desperately to end it all, but I knew that would be impossible. If I were to take my life, I would be ending my existence on earth, but I would not be ending my life. I just wanted to suddenly disappear, and no longer exist anywhere.

Since this was not possible, I felt trapped in a world I could not stand. Many nights I truly cried myself to sleep, and many mornings I woke up on the verge of tears.

> *It seemed as though I had nothing to look forward to, besides a day full of people trying to make life for me miserable.*
>
> *Over the course of time, I lost all desire for trying. Although I knew this was not good, I still could not manage to make myself try anymore."*

My parents remained committed and determined to help me. When I suggested going to a counseling center I had heard advertised on the radio, they were immediately on board.

I wrote about the experience in my journal:

> *"After listening to me describe the way my life was going, the counselor suggested that I go into the hospital for a while. At first, I agreed with her, yet after thinking about it, I changed my mind. Now, I am back to where I started from.*
>
> *A couple of days later, I visited another counselor, although I was somewhat reluctant after the first one. She did not think I needed any kind of hospital treatment, only a session once a week. I liked this idea much better than the first."*

Over time, I connected with this therapist. She offered an outlet for me to talk about whatever was on my mind. Periodically, she met separately with my parents and was especially interested in a story I had recently written.

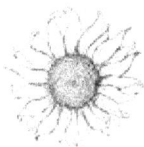

During the high school years, it is natural for best friends to grow apart. It is also quite common for one's first love not to be their last. Yet, having lost my only sibling, these losses were magnified. Experiencing Julie's death, early in life, set my context for loss.

Losing someone was to be avoided at all costs.

When faced with losing Tahlia, my best friend, and Jed, my first love who had become my closest friend, I held on as tightly as I could.

Even if it meant becoming possessive of them, and jealous of their other friendships. Even if it meant manipulating them however I possibly could.

Even if it meant threatening to end my life.

Looking back with compassion, I can see with more clarity. It felt as though I was losing my emotional support. Someone who cared for me, and understood me more than most. Someone with whom I felt like I belonged.

I did not *really* want to end my life.

I wanted a way out. To get away from the pain.

I was ill-equipped to handle the intensity of my complex emotions. It was beyond my mental capacity to comprehend how things could possibly get better.

Happiness seemed distant and unattainable.

Tahlia and Jed, each in their own way, served as lifelines for me. My parents were open to getting me the help I needed, even though my path appeared to be highly untraditional. While I do not remember talking about Julie with my therapist, she helped me process what was on the surface.

I am grateful for these influences on my life. Without them, I wholeheartedly believe, I would not have lived to tell my story.

Part Four
Below the
Surface

Begging to Be Seen

When I was sixteen years old, I penned this story. It piqued the curiosity of my therapist.

"*Through the Eyes of a Doll*

As I sit in the window, patiently awaiting someone to take me home, I notice a few girls glance at me, but they pass on by. Everyone is in a rush to get their shopping done, so no one even stops to take a good look at me.

The day comes to an end, and the store closes for the night. My friends and I discussed the day. Every night we hope that tomorrow we will find a happy home.

The very next day, a tiny girl stops to take a look. She freezes right before my eyes and glares straight up at me. Before too long, she points my way and yells for her mom to come. She anxiously hurries to see why her daughter was so excited.

I heard her call her Sally, and assumed that was her name. She begged her mom to let her take me home. My heart began to beat faster than it ever had before. My hopes began to rise, until her mother said that awful word: No.

This word raced through my head over and over again. I watched as Sally pleaded with her mother, but it was no use, her mind had been set.

Then she grabbed her daughter, by the hand, and led her through the store. I felt a tear come to my eye, as I watched them disappear. I knew right then I'd have to face another lonely day.

The store was about to close when I brushed this off as another day of sitting on a shelf. I began to wonder if I'd ever find a home besides the store. When, in the door, walked Sally and her mom.

At first I thought it was just my imagination, playing tricks on me. My hopes rose once more, as they stared at me again. I could see a sparkle in Sally's eyes, when she looked me in the eye.

After little hesitation, she picked me up and held me in her arms. I felt my heart begin to warm as she kept me close to her.

Soon, we were heading for the register. 'Could this be it? Is someone finally taking me home?' These thoughts rushed through my mind.

My questions were soon answered when we walked out the door. I peered back into the store and said a quiet goodbye to all the friends I'd left behind. I began to feel a little homesick. I wondered what my new home would be like and how I would be treated.

Sally played with me on through the night. Then, when it was time for bed, she let me sleep with her.

The next morning, when Sally and I finally awoke, she carried me down the stairs. We leisurely watched television, as she ate her breakfast. Everywhere we went that day, and for many days thereafter, she took me with her each step of the way.

Then, one night, I was sleeping with Sally, as I had always done before. But the next morning, when I woke up, she was nowhere to be found. I wondered where she could be when I heard a car leave.

I was hurt and disappointed she had left me here alone. I couldn't understand why she hadn't taken me along.

An hour or so had passed when she walked through the door. At first, I thought she would hold me, as she had in the store.

Then, I noticed she was clutching a bag in her hand. She promptly reached into the bag and pulled out another doll.

She began hugging it and holding it tightly in her arms.

A few days passed, and I watched her treat the new doll,

as she had once treated me. I longed to return to the store, for I felt so out of place.

As if this weren't enough, she tossed me in her closet along with the rest of her forgotten toys."

I do not recall my therapist asking me about this story and what it meant to me. I wonder what I would have said.

As my world evolved into new routines, did I feel like Julie was being discarded and forgotten? Or, that my emotions were being ignored or overlooked?

With the benefit of time and the depth of perspectives it offers, I find myself asking, 'Who was begging to be seen: Julie or me?'

The answer is a resounding, 'Yes!'

Taboo Feelings

Without my recollection of Julie's face or first-hand accounts of our shared experiences, she began to feel less like a sister and more like a stranger to me. She was a stranger I was supposed to know and love as much as my parents did.

Julie was perfect. I was imperfect.

These messages, and their splintered creations, were reinforced to me by my first-grade teacher and others.

Julie was the favored child. I was the one who would have been easier to give up. She was gone and I was still here, yet my parents were sad. My child-sized mind formed the conclusion: if I were gone and Julie was still here, my parents would be happy.

As I grew older, I became resentful of Julie. There was an invisible sibling rivalry between us. A competition she always won.

She was the one who rode the Pink Pig at Christmas; a childhood tradition for those living near the Rich's department store in our hometown of Atlanta. After she was gone, it was too painful for my family to take me back to ride it.

Julie was the reason I needed to "be a good little girl." Due to her extended illness and death, my parents had already been through enough.

It was my fault Julie was taken away from us.

My parents could not have handled the two of us, because I was a handful and sucked up too much attention.

She never would have veered off the path of all things good and right. She would not have gotten jealous of her friends or her boyfriend. Or, her sister.

Julie only had love for me, while I had a heap of unexpressed anger towards her. Anger for setting a standard so high, I could never measure up. Anger for stealing who my parents were before she died. Anger for leaving me behind.

She was at the center of our joyous family life.

I was the one she left to pick up the shattered pieces, which no longer formed a family of four.

I felt bad - embarrassed, shameful, and wrong - for feeling this way.

What kind of person could feel anything short of love when reflecting back on someone who has died?

I did not share my feelings with anyone. Not close friends. Not family members. Especially not my parents.

When I felt these feelings bubbling up, I ignored them. I did what I could to quit thinking about them. I moved on to whatever could best distract me.

It can be difficult for people to say anything negative about someone who has died. This is likely multiplied ten-fold when that someone is your child.

I can only imagine how much a parent longs to hold onto the memories of their child. I imagine they only have space in their memory bank for positive recollections.

Given this typical scenario, it is unsurprisingly common for a surviving sibling to feel less than or not as good as the one who is deceased.

It is not out-of-the-ordinary for a surviving sibling to feel bad for wishing their sibling would go away, disappear, or even die, and then be overcome with complex emotions when it appears their wish has been granted.

It is also normal and considered part of growing up for siblings to exchange less than kind words with each other. Naturally, the one who is left behind may feel guilty about their interactions with the one who later died.

The growing-up years can bring a plethora of arguments among siblings. This was true for Julie and me. We had our share of silent, one-sided squabbles, particularly when I was a teenager.

It felt like she had a smugness about her. She was the undisputed champion of everything that mattered.

I grew up with a well-known nursery rhyme, its author unknown, harkening back to the early 19th century:

"What are little girls made of?
Sugar and spice
And everything nice.
That's what little girls are made of."

This little girl knew she was made of things not considered nice at all. I was ashamed of being angry, especially at my sister.

I was determined not to let anyone find out what was percolating inside of me.

Visits with Death

With great consistency, my parents and I visited Julie's grave around her birthday, Christmas, and other times throughout each year.

My mom precisely arranged vibrant, plastic-stemmed flowers into the cone-shaped styrofoam, fitting into the vase attached to the rectangular marker. She took care to ensure the arrangement was appealing from every direction.

My dad brushed off the remnants of leaves, which had accumulated since our last visit. This cleared the way for the embossed details, with Julie's full name and the dates of her birth and death, to be entirely visible.

I was always reminded Julie was not there.

We were not visiting her, only where she had been buried. She was in heaven with Jesus.

We did not linger at my sister's grave.

As I grew older, my parents and I sometimes wandered around the cemetery, looking at the other grave markers. We always marveled at those who died at a young age.

When my sister died, I did not fully grasp the concept of death. It was not until seven years later before I personally knew someone who died.

Growing up, I spent an abundance of time with my relatives, who were two generations ahead of me. My grandparents and a great aunt and uncle lived near each other in the same mobile home park, about five miles from where I lived.

From an early age, I was taught to respect my elders. This meant listening to their stories and hearing about their long list of ailments. I learned to show an interest, even when as a small child, I was less than interested.

My great uncle did not hear very well, which caused him to be less engaged in conversations. He came across as a jovial man and was known for his pencil drawings of horses.

Almost every time we visited him, he drew a horse on whatever scrap of paper he could find. As a young girl, this was not enough to consistently capture my attention.

When I was 10 years old, my great uncle died.

The last time I went to visit him and my great aunt, I chose to play outside with a friend. I felt guilty and ashamed of my decision. I did not share these feelings with anyone.

Fast forward to one early morning when I was sixteen. A good friend, who I worked with, called me at home. When I answered the phone, I barely recognized her voice. She was sobbing uncontrollably. When she tried to talk, there was very little sound.

She managed to get a few words out of her mouth, each one after an extended pause.

"Deanne...is...dead."

My friend, along with Deanne, were both my age and went to a school across town. Deanne and I also went to the same church. We were close acquaintances.

I later heard Deanne had just broken up with her boyfriend and was driving home. She collided head-on with a vehicle traveling in the opposite direction. She died instantly.

It was a somber time at our church. For a little while. I wondered why people quit talking about her.

Did it really happen? Or, was it something I dreamed up? Why was I the only one who remembered?

I started to second guess my reality.

A few years later, death hit closer to home.

Throughout my growing-up years, my grandparents were at the heart of our family gatherings, both big occasions and small ones.

I also spent a lot of time with just the two of them. Whether it was riding home with them after church, going to the grocery store, or eating ice cream in a special bowl at a particular time in the evening - moments with them were far from mundane.

My granddad loved to build things out of scrap wood in his shed behind their home. I was genuinely impressed with how he could make popsicle sticks and other disposable objects into decorative windmills and other farm-themed structures.

When I headed off to college, my grandmother became my most frequent pen pal. Every chance I got to return home, which was nearly every weekend, I incorporated a visit to see her and my granddad.

During finals week, at the end of my freshman year, my granddad became ill and was hospitalized. I had never before known either of my grandparents to be admitted for overnight care. I returned home from college as quickly as I could.

For the next couple of weeks, my grandmother and I made a daily trek to the hospital to be with him. He was in intensive care, so we took turns, along with other family members, to visit him.

After what seemed like both a long and short stay in the hospital, my granddad died.

At his funeral, the pastor read a letter I had written about my granddad. Everyone who attended had a view into how much he was loved. I knew this would have made him proud.

My granddad was the first close family member I lost as an adult. His funeral was the first time I saw my grandmother cry.

Seven months after his death, I wrote a paper titled, 'My Grand Granddaddy,' which includes this passage:

> *"No one can fully understand the sorrow one is forced to withstand when a loved one is faced with death. I'll never forget the horrible feeling when the doctor confronted our family with the news.*
>
> *Though the news came as no surprise, it did not make it easier for us to hear. Somehow those words sent the message loud and clear that death happens to everyone.*
>
> *Before, and even during, Granddaddy's brief illness, I assured myself that death only happens to other people, not anyone close to me, not anyone that I love."*

Death was all around me, and yet it was rarely the topic of conversation. It was hidden in plain sight. Seen, yet not seen. Known, yet unknown.

During our visits to the cemetery, the focus was on getting the flowers into the vase on Julie's grave. While I do not recall many tears being shed there, by either of my parents or me, it was an element of our collective grieving process.

When my great uncle died, it planted the seed for the belief: choosing to play is the wrong decision. This left me with a large lump of regret.

I did not want anyone to know about the discomfort I held inside, so I secretly carried this burden with me.

It caused me not to talk about him.

What if I had shared the pain I felt inside?

What if I had known my preference for play was both normal and understandable?

What if I had compassion for ten-year-old me?

Deanne was the first person I knew who was my age when she died.

There were varying accounts of what led to Deanne's car crash in the wee hours of the morning. I do not know the whole story of what happened. I do know how distraught one could be after breaking up with someone.

My granddad's death was different from any others I had experienced. For the first time in my life, I felt like I had closure with the person who died.

A couple of months before he became ill, my granddad made several new wooden creations. He walked me through his personally crafted art exhibit, pointing out the various details to me. I was authentically interested.

He smiled a string of smiles from deep within. I felt confident he realized he mattered.

When my granddad died, and for quite a while after, I got to see my grandmother's grief up close.

She cried lots of tears. This was the first time I had seen this type of expression be such an integral part of the grieving process.

Losing her partner for the past fifty-five years impacted her daily life in a myriad of ways. From going to the grocery store to living alone in the home they had shared, there were reminders of him everywhere.

I made a conscious effort to talk about my granddad. As often as possible, I used his name at family gatherings.

I was determined he would not be forgotten.

Getting Hooked

Through being part of a girlfriend-boyfriend relationship with Jed, I knew how it felt to have someone reciprocate my love and affection.

It was a wonderful feeling. One I had never had before in this way. I wanted to feel that way again.

This accelerated my interest in guys, the older version of boys. I was always either dating someone or pursuing someone I wanted to date.

Dating was fun.

Dating was gratifying.

Dating was a distraction from my life.

After dropping out of high school, I poured my sudden discretionary time into my work at a children's clothing store. I quickly shifted from part-time to full-time status and was promoted to a role on the management team.

As a sixteen-year-old I had responsibility for opening and closing the store, merchandising, and handling periodic inventory counts. I was the go-to person for employees as well as customers.

I thrived on being able to make people's day.

When a customer was disappointed not to find her son's size in a bomber jacket he wanted, I found a way to get one delivered to our store, even though it was Christmas Eve. She was ecstatic and thanked me profusely.

Working was fun.

Working was gratifying.

Working was a distraction from my life.

By putting in full-time hours, I earned a steady paycheck. Without all of the adult obligations, it was a sizable amount of money.

I soon discovered a specialty clothing shop a few doors down from where I worked. It was a convenient stop on my way to work or when headed home for the evening.

Whenever I fell in love with one of their new arrivals, I trained myself to be patient. I learned the rhythm of their mark-downs and knew the price would be reduced in a week or two. I waited and waited, then pounced, and clinched the best possible deal.

This earned me bragging rights when showing my bag of bargains to my parents, or whoever else showed an interest.

Shopping was fun.

Shopping was gratifying.

Shopping was a distraction from my life.

Having had a taste of love, I craved more of it. I had fallen in love with the idea of being in love.

For the first time in my life, I had a leadership role with a title and was responsible for people other than myself. I knew I was making a difference.

Work, with its many payoffs, swiftly introduced me to shopping, which earned me accolades for finding bargains.

Dating. Working. Shopping. Each gave me an exhilarating buzz. One I started to seek more and more. It felt good, and I needed something to make me feel good.

Part Five
Bypassing

An All-Consuming Trio

For the remainder of my high school years and early college, I had no shortage of love interests. Sometimes, the level of interest was mutual, other times it was significantly off balance.

My relationships ranged from a single date to informal marriage proposals to a six-year marriage.

Some of those I coupled up with were loving and nurturing. Others were verbally abusive, with their personal attacks increasing in severity. More than once, these endearing and harrowing descriptors were shared by the same person. In one relationship, I found myself fleeing for my physical and emotional safety.

Being partnered up was a high priority for me.

Once I learned a certain guy liked me, it was enough of a reason for me to like him back.

He quickly went from not being on my radar to being someone I was willing to leave college for - two-thirds of the way into my sophomore year.

Months later, at the age of twenty, I got married.

I wished Julie could have been part of my wedding. It had been a long time since I could genuinely articulate missing her.

During most of my marriage, we both worked and took a full-time load of college classes. I had prior experience being a non-traditional student. A few months after dropping out of high school, I had enrolled in 'open campus' where classes were offered in the evenings.

After taking a couple of additional courses in the summer, I returned to my high school for my senior year to take a half-day worth of classes. I spent my afternoons working at a shoe store where I had been promoted into a lead role.

Months after graduating from college, the two of us separated. Six months later, we divorced. I was the first in my family to ever get divorced. It was not a title I had aimed to achieve.

I felt like a failure.

I wondered how things would have been different had Julie still been alive.

What would she have observed?

What advice would she have offered?

Would she have talked me out of getting married?

I leaned into my work. It became cemented as a safe zone, a willing recipient of my time and energy. I was leading a team of thirty employees through a major corporate reorganization, and forging strong working relationships with those I needed to influence.

I felt important. People were depending on me.

As the company doubled in size, I was at the forefront of ramping up new employees. This involved a lot of travel and late-night hours of work. I was up for the challenge and thrived in bringing order to chaos.

I felt invigorated to see the results of my efforts.

Soon, I became known for going above and beyond and was rewarded with promotions, new titles, and an expanded scope of responsibilities. The harder I worked, the more praise and recognition I received.

I felt successful.

This afforded me more money for shopping.

While working at the shoe store, I had become quite adept at mentally calculating my thirty percent employee discount as new shipments arrived. Much of my paycheck cycled back to my employer.

My affinity continued for shopping, particularly when I could find items on sale at a deep discount.

When I felt happy and excited from doing a good job, I celebrated by shopping. When I felt stressed and worn out from work, I re-energized by shopping. When I had unexpected free time, I filled it up by shopping.

There was always something I believed I needed. It was an endless cycle of consumption. It consumed an inordinate amount of my discretionary time.

Dating. Working. Shopping.

All three are considered to be good, normal, and necessary for a single adult human.

I was almost always focused on one or more of these respectable addictions. The kind whose specific point of excess is difficult to distinguish.

While these may not have been classified as clinical addictions, they were slowly removing me from my life.

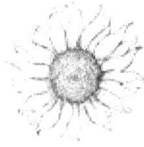

Since breaking up with my first love in high school I consistently tried to change myself to be a better fit for the relationship I was in - or was seeking.

Most times, either I was not good enough, or the other person was not good enough for me. There was always a reason not to get too close.

Based on an Australian study, which focused on how sibling loss affects development during the teenage years and beyond, this is not uncommon for those who have lost a sibling in childhood or adolescence.

"When it comes to dating, many participants avoided or experienced trouble forming relationships because they couldn't bear the pain of it not working out. Having some of those feelings of loss triggered by the failure of a romantic relationship wasn't a risk that they wanted to take" says Jan-Louise Godfrey, one of the study's researchers.

"You may end up being an only child if you lose a sibling. That was reported as being a very lonely experience. With milestones like finishing school, getting married, having a child, or as parents age, participants tended to revisit those feelings of loss. It's an enduring grief that is often revisited."

I sorely missed having a relationship with my adult sister. I wished she could offer me guidance and advice, beyond a parent's capabilities.

Throughout the course of my six-year marriage, I do not remember having many deep conversations with my then-husband. We had a superficial connection. Yet, I had grown closer with him than I had with anyone else in quite a while.

Soon after my divorce, I wrote an entry in my journal. It was a reflection on what I had written in one of my prior journals, less than a week before I met my now ex-husband:

> "*I had gone from dating one guy to the next. In the brief time that I was without a date, I wrote in my journal that I was not ready to settle down with anyone. I was dating several guys - and enjoying it.*
>
> *A few days later, I wrote that I was the same age as my mom and grandmother when they got married. I didn't have anyone in mind to spend my life with, and I was wondering, 'am I destined to be an old maid?' At 19, I was worried about that?*"

To help me process my range of feelings during my separation and divorce, I sought out my counselor from high school.

Without ever seeing this entry in my journal, she posed an observation: "I wonder if you were aiming to hurry up and recreate a family because you had lost your sister."

How could this have been true? It had been over twenty years since Julie had died. It felt almost like an excuse or a free pass she was handing me for my failed marriage.

I did not give it much thought.

With bills to pay and a new house to furnish, it was easy to stay busy with working and shopping.

Being productive and delivering quality outputs in the workplace is highly commendable. So is having a home filled with nice furniture, a kitchen fully stocked with gadgets, and lots of knick-knacks to reflect one's personality.

Embedding myself into working and shopping left little space for reflection.

I actively avoided quietness. The place where thoughts of Julie arose.

Distractions & Diversions

When I was sixteen years old, I wrote a letter to Ann Landers, a well-known advice columnist. I was hoping she could help me with a question I was struggling to answer: It has been thirteen years, why am I not over the loss of my sister?

It was a letter written in secret. I do not recall if I ever actually mailed it.

I know I never received an answer.

As I learned from my earliest memories, I quickly picked up on spoken and unspoken cues. Before I learned to read, I could sense the topic of my sister brought tearful memories and heartbreaking pain for my mom and dad. There was nothing I could do to eliminate the hurt from their hearts.

I felt helpless.

I felt a deep sadness for my sister, for my parents, and for me. I did not like feeling this way. It was dreadful and agonizing.

My goal evolved into avoiding pain.

While this was not always a conscious intention, it felt like what I needed to survive. My go-to tool was one I reverted to after my early success with Julie: making her laugh. My 'scrunchy faces' were a sure hit with my sister. And, one time when we went bowling, my mom said Julie really got a laugh out of me trying to chase the ball down the alley.

I could always be counted on to lighten the mood.

Injecting humor into tense situations is something I instinctively did when I was very young.

As I grew older, I incorporated my quick wit into various friendships, family and working relationships, and other facets of my life. If a situation could use some levity, there was a readily available, clever comment in my back pocket.

As my world expanded beyond the people who knew my sister, I was routinely asked, "Do you have any siblings?"

It was posed nonchalantly, and surrounded by inquiries like "what's your favorite color?" or "what do you want to be when you grow up?"

As a young child, I was faced with the dilemma of how to answer the deceptively simple, yet emotionally charged question of my sibling status.

To say "no" seemed to deny my sister ever existed.

To say "yes" took the conversation to a heavy place.

By the time I reached my pre-teen years, I developed a short-cut, hybrid approach as my response:

"I grew up as an only child. My sister died when she was seven and I was three. She had leukemia."

I delivered it in a matter-of-fact tone, as if reciting my well-rehearsed ABCs. I aimed to mirror the tone in which this light, get-to-know-you inquiry was presented, and render the expected short and succinct response.

I did not want the person asking the 'sibling' question to feel bad. They were unaware it would elicit any pain.

I wanted to avoid falling into a sinkhole of sadness, for myself and for those around me. I preferred to move on, as quickly and unscathed as possible, from this commonly asked question with an uncommonly complex answer.

It made me different when I was trying my hardest to be like everyone else.

Hmm...how to redirect. It was a situation ill-fitted for humor, and my heart was hurting too much to shift directly to a funny one-liner.

Out of necessity, I honed another skill: changing the subject.

From my observations, I learned people typically love to talk about themselves. When I could get the other person talking, I was expected to say very little.

After briefly sharing about my sibling situation, I would sometimes say, "tell me about *your* siblings." Since, in my complete childhood, I never came across someone with an answer like mine, it was a sure-fire way to propel the focus off of me and my loss. Once this led far enough away from the original topic, I re-engaged in the conversation.

Being likable was important to me.

People like to be happy, and people like happy people. Armed with this knowledge, gained through exposure to others, I added silver linings to my expanding skill set.

I could offer a quick fix or a handy reframe for difficult situations. Gradually, I developed a penchant for finding the light in any darkness.

This included the loss of my sister.

Many times, I was parroting back statements said to me about my unfortunate sibling status, which began with the same two-word phrase:

At least I was really young.

At least I don't have any painful memories of my sister.

At least I did not lose a parent.

Through these workarounds, my conscious thoughts of Julie were dwindling and becoming more sporadic.

Some of the distractions and diversions I developed were highly intentional, others were a natural reaction to move me beyond the situation in front of me.

After delivering witty one-liners in the midst of difficult working environments, I would often say: "Laughter is more socially acceptable than crying." While shared with a chuckle, it is disturbingly true.

Humor is a proven connector.

It can also side-track a conversation going in a direction that may be uncomfortable, yet necessary.

Changing the subject keeps the conversation flowing. By steering and shifting away from certain topics, we can preserve our sanity.

It can also prevent the conversation from running very deep, and make it easy to hide and not be seen in our struggle. This keeps us from acquiring the help we may desperately need.

Finding the silver lining is admirable, and can position us to be deeply grateful.

It can also block important feelings that need to be expressed. Eventually, we may consciously forget what we were initially trying to avoid.

I became a self-taught expert at the art of distraction and diversions. Over time, I became more and more adept at protecting myself and others from pain. My preferred way of living was sunny side up - all the way.

Losing my sister was not something I could control. My tools of the trade were designed as a means for giving me control over something. Anything.

Maybe then, I could finally be 'over' Julie.

Adulting

In my mid-twenties, and newly divorced, I moved into a newly built house. I had purchased it on my own and chosen the layout and design features.

It was a highly fitting time, as I was also rebuilding my life. Learning to live alone. Learning to take care of my own needs. Learning to speak up for myself.

I was truly becoming an adult. One who forms their own opinions and beliefs, and takes ownership of their life.

Self-development became my new pastime.

I read countless books and took several courses, focused on relationships with one's self and with others. I was determined to learn from the mistakes which led to my 'bad marriage' and to grow into the person I had always wished I could be.

Once I was settled into my own home and a new way of being, I re-entered the dating scene. The men I attracted were caring and kind.

Marriage was the last thing I wanted. I knew firsthand how painful it was when it did not work out. When my family asked about my plans to remarry, I shared a common refrain, "I would rather be alone than be with the wrong person."

As I was letting go of artifacts from my six-year marriage, I came to the realization: for as long as I could remember, I had been searching for someone who would 'complete' me.

If unchecked, I knew this could lead me back to a painful place. I declared to myself, and to a close friend for accountability, "I am not going to date anyone, or even think about someone to date, for six months."

During this time, I delved deeper and deeper into my personal growth. I continued to read and take continuing education classes aimed at discovering more about who I am and what I enjoy. I also gained clarity around the type of people I want in my life.

This purposeful pause yielded lasting dividends.

Soon after my sabbatical from dating, I found my soulmate. It was a description I had never uttered before. I had believed it to be far-fetched, if not a completely imaginary concept. From our very first date, we connected on a deep level.

When telling about our families, he shared about his mother, who died when he was 10 years old.

My heart ached for him, and for what it must have been like to grow up without his mom.

I responded, "I could not imagine losing someone so close to me at such a young age."

My response was genuine.

It was a verbal reflection of what had been happening slowly and consistently across the twenty-plus years since my sister's death.

I had grown detached from Julie.

Unexplainable Pain

I found the love of my life and we soon married. We had quickly become best friends, yet retained our personal identities.

We were helping each other continue to heal from prior relationships and accept deep and lasting love from an intimate partner.

Less than two years into our marriage, we had a unique opportunity to travel to Bulgaria. It was a trip with my husband's extended family where we explored a collection of the country's provinces.

When our travels led to a monument with a lengthy flight of stairs, his 80-year-old great aunt and I stayed on the tour bus. We were the only ones, even among those in their seventies, who did not have the energy or stamina to climb it.

During another part of our visit, we walked from one spot to another as musicians were playing their country's national anthem. Tears came to my eyes. I did not understand why. I had never cried for my own national anthem. And, it was not like me to show such emotion, especially in public.

Within three months after returning home, I began having unexplained, debilitating physical pain. I barely had enough energy to get through a regular workday and my weekends were mostly relegated to laying on the couch.

While seeking a simple solution, I read various books; this was in the days before prominent medical sources were readily available online. One book, which had been written by a reputable doctor, included a detailed assessment. It assigned the 'real' age of a person, based on their responses. The results showed I was eight years older than my biological age. I was disappointed and surprised and became more committed to resolving my pain.

My husband and I sought doctors in just about every specialty imaginable, from rheumatology to endocrinology to neurology to natural healing. Each had a different diagnosis with a common thread: the disease, disorder, or condition had no specific causes and no known cures.

I tried multiple treatments and medications to alleviate the symptoms and was not getting any relief.

Fortunately, my boss allowed me to work when I could and take care of my job responsibilities from home as much as I needed.

I used all the energy I could muster to work through the pain, so I would not have to go out on disability. I feared this option would leave me isolated from my esteemed colleagues. I already felt out of place when I went to the office and saw my co-workers engaged in exciting new projects. They were thriving with the deadlines and fast pace accompanying it, while I was barely getting by.

Each evening, I was literally crawling up the stairs to reach the bedroom my husband and I shared. I was no longer the young, healthy woman I had always known myself to be.

I felt horrible.

I did not see any end in sight for the physical pain I was experiencing all day every day.

My husband and I desperately wanted to find the root cause of my constant, full-body aches and accelerating lack of energy. After additional tests turned up nothing of substance, two separate doctors concluded I would have this pain for the rest of my life.

They each recommended I seek the help of a pain management specialist to try to make it possible to have some semblance of a normal life. It was extremely disconcerting.

Why can't they figure out what is wrong with me?

Why can't they fix my pain?

How can I possibly live like this?

I had been suffering from difficult-to-pinpoint pain, increasing in intensity, for nearly two years, and already felt like I was at the end of my rope.

I was in my early thirties and being told this is what I could expect in the years ahead of me.

This is *not* the life I wanted.

Once again, I felt as if there was no way out of my agonizing pain.

Yet, one thing was remarkably different from all of my prior encounters.

This time, my suffering was not in response to difficult emotions. It was physical pain.

Part Six
Befriending

An Emerging Possibility

After extensively searching for the reason behind my debilitating and nearly unbearable pain, and coming up short, I was exhausted.

Enduring the pain, rather than eliminating the pain, appeared to be the only remaining option. I felt like taking the prescribed route of seeing a pain management specialist meant I was giving up on ever feeling good again.

If I was going to be able to withstand the chronic, life-long physical pain, I knew I would need emotional support.

I decided to seek a professional counselor.

After a brief search, I found Mary, a licensed marriage and family therapist. On my first visit to see her, she asked me why I was there.

It was an obvious question, yet I had not prepared an answer. I responded, while thinking out loud, "I am not sure. I am a happy person. I have a wonderful, loving husband, a good family, a job I enjoy, and am about to move into a new house."

I also told Mary I was in significant physical pain.

So much so, I explained, my husband and I were moving to a new house where our living quarters would be primarily on one level. I continued by sharing about my difficulty in navigating the stairs at our current house, due to my persistent, all-over pain and lack of energy.

Mary listened closely, then asked a basic, get-to-know-you question, "Tell me about your parents and any siblings."

After letting her know my parents were still happily married to each other, I proceeded to use the well-worn statement I had recited countless times before, "I grew up as an only child. My sister died when she was seven and I was three. She had leukemia."

I braced myself for the highly predictable response I had been accustomed to receiving across many years.

After giving me a sad, distraught-looking facial expression, the person would typically say, "That must have been hard on your parents. At least, you were too young to understand."

These words were spoken by people trying to be empathic, people trying to make the situation better, and people trying to quickly move on to the next topic of conversation.

This left me feeling isolated and minimized.

There was empathy for my parents, but none for me. Early on, I learned about the varying degrees of loss. Losing a child or parent ranks high, losing a sister - especially at such a young age - does not even make the radar.

Mary had a wildly different reaction to the script I had used for decades. For the first time in my life, the person at the other end of the conversation extended empathy to *me*.

She asked me to tell her more about my sister.

At that moment, it was as if my experience was all that mattered. Using a natural, conversational flow, she posed a blend of clarifying and intentional questions aimed at going deeper.

By the end of our first session, Mary shared with me, "While I cannot promise you anything, I believe you are suffering from 'stuck grief.'"

Stuck. Grief.

I had never heard of this.

How could Julie's death - from thirty years ago - be profoundly impacting my life now?

With these two words, Mary was bringing my loss center stage, after it had long been concealed. In all my searching and researching, I had never looked for a book, class, or anything about grief. It had not even crossed my mind.

I did not immediately jump in to join Mary in her conclusion, yet I was not actively resistant to the idea.

I did not know *how* I felt. I only knew I wanted to find relief from my pain.

When Mary proposed we do some grief work together, it seemed like a recommendation with minimal risk to pursue. Her offer represented something I was yearning for: Hope.

Owning My Loss

During an early session with Mary, we excavated two of my long-held, hidden beliefs.

Both beliefs were directly contributing to my 'stuck grief.' They had become ingrained as a result of Julie's extended illness and death.

The people who initially brought them into my tiny toddler world were not bad people with ill intent - quite the opposite. These beliefs came from those who cared the most about me, as well as those who were mere passersby in my young life.

Who knows where these beliefs originated. These were beliefs *they* held tightly as well, so much so, many would describe them as facts rather than beliefs.

The first belief stemmed from the statement, "That must have been hard on your parents." On its surface, it is painstakingly true. Yet, it undermines and hinders the realization: losing my sister was hard on *me*.

The second belief was cemented by the expression: "At least, you were too young to understand." There is a kernel of truth to this statement as I was unable to verbally articulate the complex feelings that occur when losing a loved one.

At the same time, I was *not* too young to form a strong and solid bond with my sister, and to feel deep sorrow in her sudden and permanent absence.

While these beliefs protected me in some ways - unless and until they were brought to the surface - I was unable to grieve for my sister.

I had always viewed Julie's death as a loss for my parents and had never realized it was *my* loss too.

Mary listened and asked deliberate questions, which helped me to access my thoughts, feelings, and emotions from deep within. She extended empathy in a way I had never before been able to receive.

She also lovingly and assertively shared, "No one gets a pass on grief."

I felt validated at the heart level.

No one gets a pass on grief.

Not even a three-year-old.

Comparison can be the thief of grief.

When measuring our loss in contrast to others, it becomes easy to minimize our experience. We may feel unworthy of grieving. In extreme cases, it can serve as a barrier to the grieving process. And, we can find ourselves stuck.

I am grateful to Mary for jump-starting my journey of consciously processing my grief. By creating an environment to hold space for me and my myriad of emotions, I could be witnessed and acknowledged for my life-changing loss.

On that first fall day in Mary's office, I took the very first steps down the path of embracing the loss of my sister as my own.

I could already feel my heart beginning to soften.

Free-Flowing

Through my intense work with Mary, I shared what I knew about my sister and what it was like growing up without her.

This was new territory for me. I had never had a direct conversation about this with anyone.

The pain and feelings associated with my loss of Julie were buried so deep, I no longer had any conscious awareness of them.

Through weeks and weeks of therapy, I came to realize my grief is just as important as my parents' grief. And, I was, indeed, old enough to have known and loved Julie, personally, in our three short - yet full - years together.

This new understanding developed roots as I watched the interactions of a blonde-haired, blue-eyed, three-year-old cousin who looked like I did at that age.

I had no doubt she would know if her beloved grandparents were not around anymore, or if she had lost her partner in pajamas. I became keenly aware: I had suffered an incredible loss at a very young age.

I allowed, even encouraged, myself to cry. I gave voice to a multitude of secondary losses I experienced as a result of Julie's early death. I wrote in my journal:

I cry for many reasons.

I cry because of the sister that I knew and the sister that I never knew.

I cry because I know there will always be a hole in my life that only she could fill.

I cry because of the 'inside jokes' that I know we would have had.

I cry because of all the things I would have learned from her, but never had the chance.

I cry because of the sibling arguments we would have had.

I cry because I am happy to be learning more about her.

I cry because I know that I will never know everything about her.

I cry because of the experiences that I have had that would have been much more special if I would have had her to share them with.

I cry because she is not here to meet my husband.

I cry because I will never know what she would have done with her life.

I cry because my life has forever been changed.

I cry because I feel her in my heart.

In many ways, it was if Julie had just died. My grief was fresh and raw. I wept. I sobbed. I wailed.

My heart was overflowing with pent-up emotions.

I cried what felt like oceans of tears. Both in volume as well as their rushing, wave-like onset crashing onto the scene in a particular moment.

Early in my grieving process, my mom and I took a day and looked at our own slideshow of Julie and me together. I saw, firsthand, how much she and I were a part of each other's lives, and how much we loved and cared for each other.

I felt the closeness of our relationship as siblings.

With each photo, the loss of my sister became much more real. While emotionally draining and heavy at times, it was a cherished part of my healing.

In the weeks that followed, I discovered more about Julie. My dad shared a cassette tape with her reading a book.

It was a treasure being able to hear my sister's voice, especially knowing I had been a primary member of her doting audience.

My mom gave me a twenty-seven-page letter she had written to me about Julie. It was truly a gift, as it helped me to learn more about my sister and what she was like.

One thing stood out: she was not always perfect.

Julie instantly became more human and relatable.

Also, her favorite song was 'Delta Dawn,' sung by Tanya Tucker. It brought a sense of connection to know we share a love of music with rich lyrics. This song became an integral part of my grieving process. Once, my husband and I went to the cemetery and played it at Julie's grave.

On many occasions, I listened to it on repeat. Each time releasing more tears. Tears that had been waiting to come out for decades.

I was no longer stuck. My grief was flowing freely.

My lack of personal memories of Julie had seemingly offered proof for why my loss did not matter.

How can I be impacted by losing my sister when I have no memories of her?

Because my heart remembers.

In Good Company

With my newfound realization of the significant loss I had experienced, I became extremely interested in reading whatever I could find about sibling loss.

There was only one book that filled this void for me. The book, *The Empty Room*, was written by Elizabeth DeVita-Raeburn, whose older brother died when they were both teenagers.

She shared her story in a way that awakened the grief within my heart:

> "The first and biggest hurdle for me was coming to understand that my brother's illness and death had happened to me, too.
>
> For years I had been told it was my parents' loss that mattered.
>
> I had to be strong for them, make it up to them. They had already lost so much...

Slowly, I began to realize that I had suffered a profound loss and that it had been every bit as shattering as my parents' loss had been.

Everyone had seemed to understand their loss.

But no one had understood mine. Including myself."

The little, blonde-haired girl, who wanted to be seen, had finally been seen. In describing her own experience, the author was describing mine.

In the course of writing her book, she interviewed numerous people who had lost a sibling.

Given this, she wrote:

"What amazes me, when I talk to other surviving siblings, is that this theme - that the loss is not theirs to mourn - is at the core of most of their stories.

There is a definite pattern.

The parents of those who had been children at the time of the loss were often too ravaged by their own grief to recognize it in their surviving children. Nor, apparently, had there been others outside the family to recognize it and step in."

When reading these words, I felt a real and authentic camaraderie of sorts.

I no longer felt alone in my experience.

As I continued reading, I came across where DeVita-Raeburn wrote:

"Validation is in short supply when a sibling dies.

In the broad-based group I spoke with, the ultimate equation was simple: the less validation, the more ambiguous the loss, the more frozen the grief.

The younger the person was when he lost a brother or sister, the greater the ambiguity of the loss, the more frozen he tended to be.

Regardless of age, the result, in the majority of cases, was this: The loss hadn't been recognized, and the siblings hadn't grieved."

These words spoke directly to me. It was as if they were describing my own, personal circumstances. While substantial emotional labor was ahead of me, I felt in good company.

As I read further, I found an answer to a question, which had started percolating within:

Why did my grief choose to reveal itself now?

DeVita-Raeburn interviewed Pleasant White, Ph.D., who lost her only sibling to cancer when they were both teenagers. She became a therapist specializing in helping adults who lost siblings as children.

When asked about her clients, Dr. White shared:

"*A huge percentage of them come into therapy depressed and they don't think it has anything to do with the loss of their sibling.*

It usually doesn't hit until around mid-life. And there's usually a trigger, like their children reaching the same age the sibling had been, or another loss, like a divorce."

When asked about the reason for the delay, Dr. White responded:

"*Repression only works if you have the energy for it.*

When there's a lot going on in your current life and you have to redirect your energy to respond to it, the repression sometimes lifts quite suddenly."

My divorce had been an incredible loss.

I lost my primary relationship. I lost my personal identity. I lost the vision I had for my life. It was a major disruption to my core beliefs and personal values.

More recently, I had suffered a devastating and highly stigmatized loss. It occurred less than a year before that day on the tour bus in Bulgaria - where my energy level matched one of an 80-year-old woman's.

It was a family trauma, stemming from inappropriate behavior. Over the days and weeks that followed, it erupted into a complete disturbance of my family.

I was at the center of it because it had happened to me. And, I chose to speak up. My husband fully supported me, yet my family did not know how to handle it. I was expected to get over it and move on as if it had never happened.

That was not something I could do.

I felt betrayed and admonished by those I held dear to me.

I expended a deep well of energy trying to gain understanding, acceptance, and support. And, suffered through a barrage of losses: shattered holiday and celebratory traditions, the harmonious rhythm of the family dance, the way things had always been.

This emotionally charged experience, requiring the last morsels of energy I could muster, was the likely trigger for my downward spiral. One leading to sheer and utter exhaustion, and ultimately, chronic and debilitating physical pain.

My unexpressed grief, accumulated over the course of thirty years, had suddenly become a burden too heavy for me to carry.

Decades of unprocessed grief caught up with me.

With each loss I experienced, it took more and more energy to suppress my grief. Over time, it began to trickle into other areas of my life.

My lack of energy, while on the tour bus in Bulgaria, was the first time I had physical symptoms far from the norm for someone my age. During the same trip, I experienced another first for my adult life: crying and having absolutely no idea why.

At the time, I brushed off these experiences.

I lacked awareness for what they represented: whispers of grief begging to be expressed.

When first coming to terms with the grief I had buried deep inside, DeVita-Raeburn's book, *The Empty Room*, offered validation and gave voice to what was in my heart. She fueled my hope for the journey ahead.

Breakthrough Beliefs

In order to fully own my loss, I needed to revisit more of my long-held beliefs.

Over the years, I had internalized the reaction to my sibling status and started to believe Julie's death was not my loss to grieve. And, somehow, I had been too young to be impacted. This led me to formulate a statement I repeated so much, I began to believe it: I grew up as an only child.

These beliefs were joined by other generic, yet prevalent, ones:

Time heals all wounds.

Get over it and move on.

Keep your feelings to yourself - especially 'bad' emotions like anger, fear, and sadness.

I had taken such beliefs as a makeshift blueprint for how to handle loss. Emotions were meant to be fixed or flattened, rather than fully felt.

In deconstructing these deeply rooted beliefs, I simultaneously released the pressure of living up to unrealistic expectations.

Finally, I could see the truth. I did not grow up as an only child. I grew up as a surviving sibling.

The passage of time does not heal all wounds. Grieving helps us heal. We do not 'get over' those we love. We go 'through' grief, and will always carry our loved ones in our hearts.

Feelings find a way to be expressed. It is important to feel our feelings, and verbalize them when needed. Emotions wish to be acknowledged as they flow through us, and offer pathways to greater awareness.

In addition to revisiting my beliefs, I formed a couple of new, overarching beliefs.

The first was one Mary shared with me during our initial conversation: *No one gets a pass on grief.* No matter how old or young we are at the time. We all need to grieve our losses.

My other new belief: *Loss is personal.* Every loss we encounter is different than the one before. And, each person's experience and reaction to loss is unique.

We all grieve in our own way. It's less important *how* we grieve, and more important *that* we grieve.

Owning my loss, excavating and assessing my beliefs, and allowing my emotions to flow freely were all new for me.

I was already getting tangible results.

My body was happy for me. It had gotten my attention. The 'you will have this for the rest of your life' pain had served its purpose. My physical pain disappeared within a matter of months. And, my energy returned.

This was nothing short of amazing to me, as well as those who had been aware of my struggle.

How could my pain be gone so quickly? Could it have all been in my head?

Nope. It was all in my heart.

I was in the early stages of learning an invaluable life lesson: The power of grieving well.

Changing a single, commonly hidden, belief can make all the difference. When brought to the surface, we can consciously decide if it is still serving us.

Some beliefs, as in my experience, can infiltrate our lives, and permeate:

Our level of self-awareness.

Our feelings of self-worth.

Our relationship to ourselves and others.

By consciously choosing our beliefs, we free up energy better suited for healing our hearts. I am not implying all physical pain is caused by grief or even a perilous belief. What I know for sure is my physical pain kept growing in intensity and became the center of my life.

It was the primary topic of conversation with well-meaning family, friends, and co-workers aiming to offer a solution. It was eclipsing my go-to escape mechanisms: working and shopping. And, it threatened to be a constant third-party intruder in my relationship with my soulmate.

I was truly 'stuck' and unable to move forward.

My therapist gave me the gift of care and compassion, along with a neutral position. In this sacred space, I did not need to expend energy trying to avoid causing hurt feelings or heartbreak. I could focus my efforts on exploring the unfiltered story of my life.

The sudden disappearance of my pain was my body's way of signaling to me: My heart was beginning to heal.

I was opening up to grief.

Part Seven
Blossoming

Reclaiming
a Gift of Love

For as long as I can remember, I have known the dates of two key milestones in my sister's life and in my family's life: The day Julie was born and the day she died.

Some years, on these specific dates, her name has merely been mentioned as a fact with little emotion. "This was Julie's birthday. She would have been x years old." Or, "This is the day Julie died - x years ago."

Other years, these dates have sparked a conversation about who she was or how she died. At times, they lead to a series of 'what ifs' about who she would have become.

I wonder what Julie would have been like if she had lived longer.

Would she continue to be confident and outgoing?

Would she have gone to college? Would she have a career? If so, what would she have chosen? Would she have gotten married? Had children of her own? Become a grandmother?

I wonder what my parents would have been like had Julie lived longer.

Would they have given us more or less attention as individuals? How would my parents have been 'broken in' by my sister? What restrictions would they have put into place *because* of her?

I wonder how my life would be different with Julie physically in it.

Would I have been happier as a child? Would I have been so shy and quiet? Would I still be described as 'wise beyond my years'?

I wonder how our sibling relationship would have evolved over the years.

Would we have remained the best of friends? What silly things would we have fought over? What inside jokes would we have?

These are questions without answers.

While we can all speculate, based on our own hopes, biases and beliefs, no one truly knows.

After coming to terms with my sister's death being a very real part of my life's journey, it sparked my desire to do something to honor her memory.

In a quiet moment during my morning commute to the office, it came to me: I could donate my hair.

While my sister was enduring chemotherapy treatments, clumps of her hair started coming out rather quickly. In the mid-1970s, there were very few options for wigs. Most were wiry, made of a synthetic material rather than human hair, and geared towards adults. This made a distressful situation even more difficult.

What must it have been like for Julie to experience losing clumps of her hair? Or for my mom, who combed and styled my sister's hair each day?

By donating my thick and healthy hair, I hoped I could help alleviate one child's angst around the unavoidable prospect of losing their own hair during treatment.

On what would have been Julie's fortieth birthday, I donated a foot of my hair to be crafted into a wig for a child with cancer. This was the culmination of over two years of actively growing my hair to serve this purpose.

It marked an intense time of processing my grief through a series of sessions with a caring therapist, countless conversations with my husband, and meaningful interactions with my parents.

When the day arrived, it felt like such a release.

At last, I could do something to tangibly acknowledge the impact Julie has had on my life while paying it forward to a child in need.

I believe she would be proud.

After my life-affirming haircut, my husband and I headed to our home to spend the afternoon with my parents.

We enjoyed a birthday cake decorated to celebrate Julie's life on her special day and planted a hydrangea in our backyard as a remembrance of her.

My parents presented me with two packages.

The first was a small album with muted yellow and orange plaids on a white background, adorned with three yellow buttons on the front. As I opened up the front cover, I found the title page: My Sister & Me.

My mom and dad had thoughtfully sifted through their slides chronicling the moments shared between Julie and me, and selected about eighty of them to be converted into photos.

It touched me deeply to see Julie holding me as an infant, again and again. And, us snuggling up together in our bed when I was a toddler.

It was as if I were her very own baby doll.

I was holding living proof of our sisterly bond.

We were celebrating our birthdays, all three of the ones I shared with her, with joint parties. We were enjoying each other's company while posing in our Easter clothes or discovering what Santa Claus brought us for Christmas each year.

We were a twosome specializing in making the most of ordinary moments. Julie reading a book to me. The two of us sitting atop a wicker clothes hamper. My sister and I, her sitting and me squatting, on top of our kitchen table covered with newspaper. We were both hugging a large, oval watermelon we are about to enjoy with our parents and grandparents.

The album records the life we lived as sisters.

As we were nearing the end of Julie's time on earth, her appearance changed dramatically. Her small frame began holding more weight, a side effect from the various treatments she received. And, her long, flowing, light brown locks were replaced with a dark brown, shoulder-length wig which was obviously not her hair.

My parents also included an image I distinctly remembered from our slide show viewings in my younger years. One of Julie and me laying in bed together when she was not wearing her wig.

I am thankful my mom took this picture and included it in the album. It depicts reality.

As we perused the collection of photos, my parents shared memories of Julie and me together. I learned more about what our family was like back then.

Each page offered a heartwarming reminder of the love and adoration Julie had for me - and me for her.

It also revealed a deeply insightful discovery.

Before my sister died, a lady at our church gave us each a purse she had specially sewn for us. The purses were cloth with a single large flap on the front to contain its contents and a shoulder strap.

Julie's purse had little flowers and rag dolls printed on its deep orange background, along with red, zig-zag stitching bordering the front of its flap, which was accentuated by solid red fabric.

I do not remember what my purse looked like. Because, after Julie died, I stole her purse and carried it everywhere with me. Or, at least it was the story I had been told. The one my mom and dad both believed to be true. Until, when carefully curating photos for the album of My Sister & Me, my parents found me carrying the purse *before* Julie died.

The photos uncovered the truth.

Julie had *given* me her purse.

Once she was gone, the purse became a physical representation of my connection to her.

I took the purse with me wherever I went - when I played, when I ate, and when I slept.

What a wonderfully thoughtful gift from Julie. One that brought me comfort as only a big sister could.

A couple of years later, when I was five years old, my dad placed the purse in the top drawer of the chest of drawers in their bedroom. As he did so, he told me the purse was being put away for safekeeping and would be returned to me when I was older.

I tilted my head back and looked up, trying to catch a glimpse of my precious purse. But, the drawer was well above my head.

I was sad. I wanted my purse back.

I did not understand why I could not have it.

After taking our time perusing the photo album, on the day denoting Julie's fortieth birthday, my parents gave me the remaining package.

It contained my beloved purse. The one my seven-year-old sister gave to three-year-old me. Just as I remembered it, minus the shoulder strap. My mom said the shoulder strap was so tattered and torn they had removed it years ago, yet she wished she had left it.

This did not take away the priceless value of the best regifting experience of my life.

I genuinely appreciate my parents for capturing many of the moments Julie and I shared.

It is truly a gift to have a collection of photos of my sister and me. One I can access at any time. We now have a private space for remembering our lifelong bond, and I feel closer to Julie each time I visit.

I am grateful my parents were open to seeing the reality of what happened with my sister's purse and sharing their discovery with me. The belief that I had stolen it had made me feel a bit underhanded, as someone who takes what does not belong to them.

Knowing Julie wanted me to have her purse, leaves me feeling special and loved.

My sister gave me a part of her.

When I reflect on the day my dad put my purse away, I feel empathy. Empathy for my parents who must have been at their wits' end for what to do.

It probably seemed unhealthy for me to be carrying a possession of Julie's with me so long after her death.

I am sure my parents had many discussions about what they thought was best before they made the decision. I feel certain it was not easy to take away my purse - for good.

What neither my parents nor I knew, at the time, is - years later - the purse my sister gave me would be defined as a transitional object.

In a blog, written by Lisa Kanarek for Well+Good, she shares:

> *"Photos, videos, and shared stories can comfort those grieving the loss of a loved one member. But a more tangible item—an article of clothing, a favorite book, or, in my case, a boxy chair—can build a strong connection and make the grieving process a little less painful.*

> *'Items and objects often hold a lot of memories and experiences and bring our loved ones back to us more readily,' says Helen Marlo, Ph.D., chair of the department of clinical psychology at Notre Dame de Namur University in Belmont, California.*

> *Dr. Marlo says that you may be motivated to invest mental energy into an item, even if it doesn't hold significant meaning because you can channel your longing for the person you lost onto the object.*

> *'For a lot of people, it's evidence that the person existed, especially if the death was unexpected,' says Megan Devine, LPC, psychotherapist, and bestselling author*

of It's Okay That You're Not Okay. '*Even when the death was expected, sometimes there's that unreality like they were here, and now they're not.*'"

The photos document the journey of Julie's gift to me, and the sense of security and connection it offered. It was always by my side, much like my sister had always been.

I have empathy for myself as a little, blonde-haired girl. I wonder how I made sense of my purse being taken away.

Did it feel like I was losing another part of me?

Did I think I had done something wrong?

Is that when I started to detach from my grief?

On Julie's fortieth birthday, my family laughed and cried in each other's presence, and reclaimed a part of our collective past.

I will always treasure my little orange purse with the red border around its single flap.

And, even more so, the sister who gave it to me.

Healing through Uncertainty

After my physical pain from my pent-up grief vanished, my husband and I turned our attention to expanding our family.

We soon found out we were among the ten to fifteen percent of couples who would struggle with infertility. After two rounds of treatments, we were given low, single-digit odds of conceiving a child.

How could this be happening? We have already suffered our share of heartbreaks in this lifetime. Surely, we have met our quota of losses for a while. These, and other, distressing thoughts were racing through my mind.

This was a loss. An ambiguous loss.

One steeped in uncertainty - whether to grieve or hold out hope.

Recognizing this life-changing reality as a loss, was one hurdle. Another was recognizing the beliefs I had assumed to be facts. A family is not complete unless it includes children. The biggest joy in life is to have children. Children give your life meaning. I also had beliefs to overcome regarding my inability to conceive.

One by one, I dispelled these beliefs, replacing them with ones that affirmed my life.

While I was hyper-aware of my infertility being a loss for others, I needed to own it as *my* loss. To care for me as if I had just suffered a devastating, heart-wrenching loss. Because I had.

I gave myself the grace and space to grieve.

To kindly decline the baby shower of a friend. To make my own plans for Mother's Day. To gently remind myself to breathe.

To fully feel my emotions.

To grieve what I had lost. The dream of having children. The way I thought things would be. Becoming a mother, and seeing my husband become a wonderful father. Being able to crown my mom and dad with the moniker of grandparents.

As the only surviving sibling, this was a heavily weighted burden to release.

I took the time I needed to process my grief and allowed myself to heal.

I gained empathy for those who are unable to bear children, and better understood how common daily occurrences can trigger difficult emotions. I formed connections with those who have traveled along the journey of infertility. I have shared my story, been witnessed and validated, and have done the same for others.

Gradually, I began to find meaning in the journey. And, uncovered personal insights that brought deeper understanding, and helped me continue to heal.

For as long as I could remember, I had been terrified of shots of any kind. The infertility treatments required me to receive shots in my stomach, multiple times per day, administered by my husband.

In facing my fear of the needle puncturing my skin, I acquired a new realization.

As a toddler, when Julie was screaming out in pain, I learned it was because of the shots she had gotten at the doctor's office. This simple reasoning morphed into deeply embedded anxieties I had carried with me throughout my childhood and into my adult years.

By shining light on where my fear likely originated, it helped me to let it go.

I realized how processing my grief for Julie had equipped me to be intentional in answering a common question from friends, new acquaintances, and well-meaning strangers:

"Do you have any children?"

After the rawest of my wounds had healed, I framed up a response that felt authentic and honored my journey: "We were unable to have children, and we chose not to adopt."

In sharing a sound bite of my story, I hoped to remind the person with the inquiry: having children does not happen for everyone. And, adoption was not a uniquely creative solution, which had not crossed our minds.

My greatest hope was to plant a seed to help the next person with a journey similar to mine.

I was also learning to establish boundaries about what I shared and to do so in a way that made me feel whole and complete.

I gained empathy and connection, which continued the cycle of personal insights.

Over time, I became grateful for the experience and the outcome. It brought me closer to my husband and opened us up to new and exciting dreams to pursue. And, it helped to raise my awareness that I was meant to give back to the world in other ways.

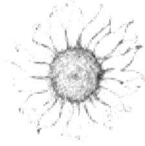

Being the sole surviving sibling added another layer of grief to my journey through infertility. I held the key to whether or not my parents would become grandparents. Their friends were talking about their adventures as newly minted grandmothers and grandfathers.

I was my parents' only hope of having their own stories to share. Because of me, they would not have grandchildren to spoil or the special relationship that comes with witnessing a child's exhilarating firsts throughout their life.

In many ways, the losses surrounding my dream of bearing a child mirrored the losses surrounding my dream of growing up with my older sister. Both were unknown or left unacknowledged by most of the people around me. With each one, I was initially more focused on it being a loss for my parents. And, I had an inner voice incessantly wondering what was wrong with me.

Gratefully, there was one profoundly important difference: I was granting myself the grace and space to fully feel and process my losses.

I was grieving well.

Tending
to Life Scars

Owning the loss of my sister was a powerful and significant step for me.

On the surface, it had been one loss. A loss that happened long ago.

In reality, Julie's death sparked an avalanche of losses that would impact every fabric of my being.

I have done a lot of grieving and healing in the years since first dislodging my 'stuck grief.' At times, it is intense. Other times, it is far from the front and center of my mind space.

There is a distinct benefit in revisiting what it was like - is like - to be a surviving sibling, now with over four decades of experience. I continue to collect insights and perspectives, leading me to understand myself even more.

Loss and its many impacts, much like a physical scar, never fully go away. While our emotional bumps and bruises can heal gradually, with a certain level of awareness and focus, their scars will always be with us. It is part of what makes us who we are.

One of the first feelings I recall ever experiencing is helplessness.

I have a mental image of Julie, laying on the couch in our living room, screaming uncontrollably in unbearable pain. Either my mom or dad was consoling her, trying to make things better. I was standing a few feet away, watching intently, transfixed by what was happening.

I do not know if this is an actual, accessible memory of mine or if my advanced brain has assembled the pieces from what I have learned about my sister and her long-term illness. In any case, there was nothing I could do. There was little, if anything, my parents or Julie could do.

I was feeling helpless, and I was surrounded by a sense of helplessness.

When Julie died, I knew it made my parents tremendously sad and deeply distressed. Once again, there was nothing I could do to make the pain go away.

I felt helpless.

Throughout my life, I have had a hard time seeing anyone in pain. This extends to physical or emotional pain, even if it is me perceiving they are experiencing discomfort. I have wanted to interrupt the cycle. Make everything okay. Relieve their suffering. At times, this has led me to help and overhelp. All in an effort to fix things.

Not everyone needed or wanted the help I provided. This can lead to a vicious cycle of exhaustion and resentment.

No matter how many people I help, for as long as I live, I can never erase the helplessness I felt from not being able to help Julie. I can take comfort in knowing I did all I was meant to do.

While helplessness is the first feeling I specifically remember, another one has evoked more of my out-of-character, shadow-side reactions than any other: Feeling minimized.

This stems from feeling unnoticed, unimportant, and unappreciated. Feeling like my feelings do not matter. And, by extension, feeling like *I* do not matter.

It could be as seemingly insignificant as an idea not being heard or being quickly discounted. Finding myself in a situation where I need to rationalize or justify my needs, or when someone is frequently unwilling to make time for me.

These scenarios could feel like personal attacks. Or, the other extreme, as if I am completely invisible.

In most cases, I have been able to hide how I was feeling inside. On a few occasions, it has unleashed a fit of rage, leaving those in its wake perplexed and confused. Including me.

Gradually, I made the subconscious shift of eliminating the intermediary and being the one minimizing myself.

I minimized my feelings. I minimized my needs. I minimized my voice. By doing so, I made myself small.

While continuing to lean into my grief, and the experience of other surviving siblings, I found the probable, original source for this difficult emotion.

I am a 'forgotten mourner.'

This term is commonly used to describe those left behind when their brother or sister dies. Or, children under the age of five when death takes someone close to them.

It is a phrase bestowed upon those who are assumed to be less affected by the death of a loved one.

When discovering the descriptor 'forgotten mourner,' I felt seen. I felt validated. I felt like there is a reason why I am the way I am.

Through awareness and intention, I am changing this long-running script.

I am learning to notice when I am feeling minimized, or being the one minimizing and letting my emotions flow through me.

I am learning to identify and find ways to consciously meet my own needs, even when it requires asking for what I need.

I am learning to use my voice to say what needs to be said. To speak up and out.

Feeling minimized is a close companion of one that rounds out the life scars from my deepest emotional wounds: Feeling on the outside.

As if I do not belong. Anywhere.

Through my grieving process, I have come to realize I am afflicted with Third Wheel Syndrome.

I thought I was the first who strung these three words together until a quick Internet search revealed its entry in the Urban Dictionary: "a disease in which no matter what group of people you're with, you're always the one left out."

Most of the related links refer to what it is like to be single among coupled friends, yet I can easily imagine this being a fitting term for anyone who feels othered in some way.

I became a third wheel at the tender and impressionable age of three. For me, it describes what it was like to suddenly become a single child in a family of three. The one who was no longer part of a duo.

My parents were a couple. Both adults, with adult responsibilities, and adult bedtimes. No matter how much they may have tried to include me in their world, I was on the outside.

By my own description, third wheel syndrome occurs when I feel like an outsider around two people who appear to have a tighter bond with each other than either of them shows an interest in having with me. This can be true in a particular moment or throughout the broader scope of a relationship.

After repeated occurrences throughout my life, it has led to a leeriness of small, odd-numbered groups. I have come to expect being the odd-person-out when people partner up, whether formally or informally.

It feels like there is no point in trying to fit in because it is painstakingly obvious I do not fit in. And yet, I still try to fit in. Expending much of my energy reserves when all I really want to do is to withdraw and isolate myself. I yearn to find a closet, suitable for the adult-sized me, where I can feel safe and secure. A place where I fully belong.

This is primarily a struggle that resides inside my being and something I typically keep to myself.

Others certainly do not intend for their subtle actions and reactions to cause such internal despair, and rarely even realize something has gone awry.

If I am not consciously careful, I can concoct a story that runs, full force, into the deepest and darkest corners of my psyche, and is only constrained by the energy I allow myself to give to it.

I am learning to get curious about my feelings, so I can continue along the pathway of deeper awareness.

I am learning to give compassion and acceptance to the woman looking back at me in the mirror.

And, to comfort the little girl who first experienced these sensations when she lost the world wrapped up in her big sister.

While I could never fully unravel the countless impacts of my sister's death, I have found it to be helpful to explore the wounds behind my scars.

Through finding out how they got there - much like knowing what happened to break one's arm - I am uncovering the stories of my life. With clarity and compassion, I can pause and check-in with myself when faced with feeling helpless, minimized, or on the outside.

I can help from a place of understanding what is actually mine to do. I can make space for myself. I can choose to be where I belong.

In doing so, I am creating a life around what fills my cup and brings me joy.

Unfurling

The loss of my sister, early in my childhood, has indelibly shaped my life

Grief and grieving opened up my capacity for more love in my days. And, changed the way I live.

How did this happen? Gradually.

What started as a pie in the sky remedy for my horrendous physical pain, quickly morphed into a journey of better understanding myself.

Understanding my loss and its far-reaching impacts. Understanding what makes me who I am.

As my level of understanding increased, the empathy I held for myself also increased. Empathy for three-year-old me. Empathy for teenage me. Empathy for adult me.

I began to experience a wider range of emotions and a fuller spectrum of feelings.

At first, this was a bit jarring.

For much of my life, I had tamped down my behavioral instincts as a means of keeping myself from stepping over the edge. Or, from going to a place where there was no turning back.

With loving support, I found the confidence and courage to access my innate, yet previously underexpressed empathy. My emotional comfort zone started to expand.

The empathy I was extending to myself began overflowing to others.

Personal stories started emerging and being exchanged more freely, leading to deeper bonds and more meaningful connections.

This fueled a steady stream of introspection, expanded awareness, and personal insights.

Setting out on the path of coming to terms with the depth and breadth of my loss, both from long ago and in the present moment, offered renewed meaning for my life.

As I travel along this journey, the soul-nourishing cycle of empathy, connection, and personal insights is continuing to unfold.

I am embracing my Inner Trailblazer as a pathway to tuning into my needs and boldest dreams, soaking up the uniqueness accompanying each season, and serving as a catalyst for connectedness.

I am remaining curious as new layers of loss reveal themselves, and offer opportunities for me to learn, grieve, and heal a little more.

On my best days, this is how I live. On most days, this is how I aspire to live more of my life.

Every day, I am unfurling further and further to unveil more of my true self, and by doing so, I am forging a deeply comforting and desirable outcome:

True belonging.

.

Growing the Distance

A few years ago, I decided to attend a structured, three-day retreat in California with other women entrepreneurs.

This was a big decision for my husband and me.

In addition to the financial investment, the dates for the retreat conflicted with our highly anticipated, and much-needed, beach vacation.

The decibel of stress and activity we were experiencing was amplified far beyond a typical year. After much contemplation, I had walked away from a quarter-century career in the corporate world, and we were adjusting our lives to the cascading impacts.

As much as we needed a vacation, we both intuitively knew I was meant to be at the retreat.

In the weeks leading up to it, the host was upfront about the possibility of transformation it held. While I did not know exactly what to expect, I was open to whatever awaited me.

I was committed to making the most of the experience. For me, this meant taking solitary nature walks and waking up early enough to simply be. This was a significant shift for me, as I gravitated towards being constantly busy and productive.

On the second morning, before the day's retreat activities began, during my moments of pause, my mind wandered to the date on the calendar.

It was the anniversary of my sister's death.

Through streaming tears of grief and joy, I tapped my feelings into my phone as quickly as they flowed:

> *"She was my first friend, the first person I made laugh, the first person I looked up to, the first person who 'got' me.*
>
> *My one and only sister.*
>
> *Then, she was gone. At least on earth.*
>
> *She became untouchable, someone who I could never be as good as.*
>
> *Someone whose goodness and perfect-ness cast a shadow over me - throughout my childhood.*

After much inner work, I learned that no one gets a pass on grief.

I learned that my grief was just as important as my parents' grief.

I learned that I was old enough to have known and loved her, personally, in our three short - yet full - years together.

For the first time in my life, I deeply and completely grieved for her.

Years later, it is now today.

Forty-four years ago, on this day, Julie became a guardian angel for me.

How fitting that I am finding out, now - and fully owning - how bright my own light is shining."

I could release my deep-rooted belief: I am supposed to act small.

I no longer needed to live in Julie's shadow. The one she cast simply by being who she was. The one I had continued to carry in her absence. Our sibling rivalry was finally and completely over.

My sister and I could coexist as wonderful people.

Worthy of being fully seen, appreciated, and loved.

In the course of writing this book, I revisited memories from my childhood, as well as the letter my mom wrote to me years ago - the one about Julie and her life. Through this process, I granted myself permission, along with the courage to 'go there' and explore the mountains and valleys coming together to make up my one-of-a-kind life.

By allowing myself to soak up the words within my mom's letter, I expanded and renewed my sense of compassion for what our family endured. It gave me a contextual foundation for the weeks immediately preceding Julie's death and the weeks that closely followed.

I had never thought about this extended timeline.

While I had read the words a handful of times before, this time, I felt them more deeply. And, for the first time ever, I deliberately offered empathy to three-year-old me for the emotional trauma brought on by this intense period of my young life.

I consciously created a quiet and peaceful environment where my feelings could flow freely.

Now, in addition to marking the day my sister died as Julie Remembrance Day, I reserve the day to feel whatever I need to feel without the pressure of structured plans. Forty-six years after my profound loss, I now set a reminder of the day weeks in advance.

It is a visual cue to grant myself an added dose of compassion, blended with the grace and space I need. To honor and acknowledge the intensity of losses my little three-year-old self experienced.

And, it brings more meaning to the low-grade, melancholy days I sometimes encounter during the month of my sister's death, around the holidays, my sister's birthday, milestones in my life, or on an ordinary day.

More and more, I am letting grief flow through me when it chooses. As well as the other emotions - anger, fear, and sadness - consistently traveling with it. They are a part of what makes me human.

Rather than judge myself while trying to figure out what is wrong with me, I am holding genuine compassion for myself and recognizing my feelings for what they are: grief and grieving.

Spreading Seeds

Early in my grief work with Mary, she told me, "When one person goes to therapy, their whole family goes to therapy." In my case, this extends to friends, co-workers, and perfectly placed strangers who cross my path.

Ever since I began fully owning the loss of my sister, and better understanding how her life and death impacts my life, I have wanted to share my journey with others. In my wildest dreams, I imagined telling my story in front of a large audience in a beautiful ballroom. I dreamed of changing the way people look at their own loss and the losses of others - one day.

A few years passed, and in 2008, my husband and I decided to create a business together. Over time, we planted grapevines, opened a tasting barn, and built a winery. We lovingly renovated an early 1900s farmhouse, an ideal getaway for those seeking a spot to rest and recharge. It is truly a labor of love.

Our mission is to offer a place to connect with nature's simple pleasures. Our team, guests, and community - many of whom are now friends - have told us we are making a positive impact. They feel like family. Even more so, they feel a sense of belonging.

The empathy I gained from owning and grieving the loss of my sister greatly influences how I show up in the world. It also amplifies my passion for mentoring: relationships built on exchanging our stories, including the ones where we are not the hero.

This led me to actualize the moment I had visualized over a decade before.

I was recognized with the 2017 Red Letter Mentor Award, from The WICT Network's Southeast Region; an informal mentee nominated me for the honor. Being a recipient gave me the opportunity to give an acceptance speech in front of an audience of hundreds of people.

I immediately knew the topic I would choose.

When receiving the award, in the large beautiful ballroom, I shared what it was like to grow up as a surviving sibling, and how, for many years, I externalized the numerous ways Julie's death had impacted me.

I told of the courage it took to dig deep within, to feel my feelings, and to grieve my sister.

I offered hope and encouragement by highlighting what had become one of the most powerful insights gained from my journey with grief:

The power of empathy. For myself and others.

It was a night I will always treasure. My husband, my parents, and others close to me were there to experience the full-circle moment. I still remember the scores of people who came to talk with me afterward. Many shared their own story of loss.

It felt good to offer healing for other hearts.

The following year, I was chosen to work on one of the company's first cross-divisional teams created to improve the employee experience. One of our primary areas of focus was to overhaul the company's policy for bereavement for over 50,000 employees. As was common in corporate environments, at the time, the original policy designated the amount of time off based on traditional, familial relationships.

We designed the new policy with empathy at the heart of it. Employees no longer need to spend energy proving how much time a particular loss warrants. They are trusted to take the time needed, so they can focus on what matters, which includes grieving their loss.

It was my last corporate project. When I had an opportunity to leave the company, I took it. It felt like a perfect ending to my corporate career.

By leaving the corporate arena, it created the space I needed for another long-held dream to come to fruition: creating my own business to guide others in traversing crossroads and turning points along life's journey.

When serving as a guide for inward explorations, I get to leverage my gifts, which include discerning nature's stories and bringing its many lessons to the forefront. Among other offerings, I have hosted personal and small group retreats focused on growing through loss and grief. It brings me joy to help others find healing, and bloom to their fullest potential.

This closely aligns with one of my core values:

We go through things so we can help others.

It deepens the meaning in our lives. Connects us to each other. And, helps us heal.

Grieving Well

I fell in love with sunflowers a long time ago. I do not recall the exact moment my lasting affection for them was sparked, but I remember it was around the time I was moving through the darkness of divorce and getting settled in my own home.

In short order, there were sunflower figurines, framed art with sunflowers, and sunflower knick-knacks displayed throughout my house. It was my undeniable decor theme.

Why do I have such a love of sunflowers?

Initially, it was a surface-level attraction. I was drawn to their uniqueness, their vibrant colors, and the way they seem to exude confidence.

My intrigue in them soon blossomed, and I became more familiar with their behaviors. Sunflowers follow the sun. They look for the light and make it their focus. In doing so, they turn away from the darkness.

It is one of the things I deeply admire about them.

For much of my life, I aimed to emulate the sunflower's above-ground orientation to what I surmised was all things positive.

Over the years, I deepened my knowledge and understanding of my favorite flower, and came to a personal revelation:

Sunflowers spend a lot of time in darkness.

They grow in nutrient-rich soil, throughout the night, even while blooming.

By facing the darkness, they can reach their full brilliance.

This inspires me to be upfront about another long-lasting relationship: the one I have with grief.

Grief was once my invisible, and not-so-invisible, friend. The friend I thought I had long outgrown and left behind.

It was leaving fingerprints all over my life, whether I realized it or not. Even when we were not on speaking terms. Even when I tried to ignore its existence.

As I learned, firsthand, grief will find a way to be seen through any means necessary. Even acting out in hurtful and destructive ways. Even if it has to disrupt my best-laid plans to get my undivided attention.

Increasing its complexities, there is not a one size fits all guidebook for grief, and countless others have also struggled with finding a proper balance in their own relationship with it. Even so, I found solace and support from compassionate souls and those further along in their journey. I came to realize, grief ultimately wants what is best for me, and has all along. It was yearning for acknowledgment and acceptance.

With courage and intention, I have transformed my relationship with grief from 'stuck' to a much more engaging and empowering one - defined as 'grieving well.'

By my personal definition, grieving well is granting ourselves the grace and space to fully feel and process our losses.

For me, this looks like tuning into my needs and nurturing myself as a loving friend. Intentionally pausing to simply breathe, leaning into caring and supportive relationships, and creating and maintaining healthy boundaries to nourish my body, mind, and spirit.

It includes reminding myself that grief is not linear, and sometimes feels like I am revisiting a wound I thought had healed. When this happens, I aim to gently accept it has a reason for what seems like turning me inside out, upside down, or going in a backward motion.

I am learning to extend myself permission to feel whatever bubbles up to the surface, unravel its intricate layers and lessons, and be open to what it reveals.

Grief comes with highs and lows, a complex concoction of emotions, and varying levels of intensity. Sometimes, it is at the forefront of my consciousness; other times, it patiently and passively waits for a better time to approach me. It lives by its own timeline.

By treating grief with reverence, its rewards are frequent and ongoing. It brings healing to my heart and strengthens my personal bonds.

As I walk alongside this friend of mine, I am delighting in its abundant return on my intentional and ongoing investment. It is guiding me to live in full color, tune into the preciousness of life, and discover moments of magic and meaning.

I value the hope it offers, as it brings me full circle: holding immense love for the sister who nurtured me as a baby and toddler.

The sister I lost too soon.

And, the sister I have found again.

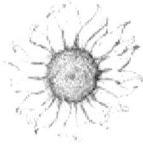

As I continue along my journey, I am carrying forward what I have found to be true:

Grieving well is a practical and beneficial life skill.

It honors ourselves and those we hold close to us, making our hearts bigger.

And, when we are ready, it brings awe-inspiring joy and lightness to our world and those around us.

By opening up to grief, we are opening up to love.

Afterword

I wrote this book to honor Julie's life and her impact on mine.

My intent is to pass along the wisdom I have gained along the journey. Having lost my sister at such a young age, part of my purpose is to validate those who wonder if they 'should be over' their loss by now.

I have been walking this path for nearly half a century, and am still learning, grieving, and healing.

Grief is a continuous thread, unraveling and revealing more of who we are. We are evolving and changing. Our loss impacts us differently at different points in our lives.

I feel blessed to be living the life I am living. I would not be where I am, or who I am becoming, without the path that led me here.

I am fortunate and privileged.

While I am sharing the story of my own journey, other survivors have had to navigate vastly different and significant struggles.

As a white, heterosexual, cisgender female, not living with a disability, who grew up with loving parents in a middle-class neighborhood, I started along this path without additional layers of access and equity. The ability to receive personal therapy, as well as the support of my soulmate, affords me benefits beyond many others who are surviving siblings before adulthood.

This realization is traveling deeper and deeper into my soul each day.

Based on a 2013 study by researchers at Yale University's School of Public Health, "experiencing the death of a sibling during childhood and early adulthood is a common phenomenon." Their findings "suggest a divergent pattern of transition to adulthood following the experience of sibling death with respect to educational attainment, establishing an independent residence, marriage, employment, and fertility."

Writing this book has reinforced why I am an advocate for grief. I am using my voice for the scores of surviving siblings who have not yet found theirs.

You are who kept me motivated when my stories had difficulty flowing onto the page.

I hope you feel seen and acknowledged. I hope you connect more deeply with the stories influencing your life. I hope you grant yourself the grace and space to fully feel and process your losses.

Maya Angelou said it best, "when you know better, you do better." We can honor our younger selves for how far we have come. We can embrace beliefs and make choices to better support where we are headed.

I hope you join me in envisioning a world where grieving is embraced as a natural part of living our lives. We each have a part to play in changing the way we look at our own loss and the losses of others.

We can educate others with our stories, and with what our hearts know to be true.

Together, we can ignite a new narrative - one in which surviving siblings are seen and acknowledged for their life-changing loss - so we can *all* get the support needed for hope and healing.

We can celebrate our progress every time one of us gazes into the mirror and honestly proclaims:

You are deeply loved - and always will be.

Acknowledgments

While reflecting, remembering, and recounting the stories from my life has been a distinctly personal experience, bringing this vision to life required a multitude of support.

My heart is overflowing with love and gratitude.

To my Creator, for making me all of who I am, for sending perfectly placed people along my path at precisely the right time, and for surrounding me with nature's love.

To Julie, for jump-starting my life with your physical presence, for leaving an indelible imprint on me, and for the sisterly bond we will always share.

To my Soulmate, for living much of this story with me, for offering pure acceptance, for being my partner in pursuing bold dreams and everything life brings, and for being the magnificent soul who sings with mine.

To my Parents, for creating our family of four and surviving with me as a family of three, for sharing your memories of Julie, and for loving me beyond words.

To my Grandmother, born a surviving sibling, for having empathy for me, for nurturing me, and for pouring 'oceans of love' on me.

To Tahlia, for being my surrogate sister, for sharing your childhood and teenage years with me, and for helping me learn about friendship.

To Jed, for being my first love, for showing me how loving a boyfriend could be, and for being in tune with what I needed at such a critical time.

To Younger Me, for writing about your feelings and preserving key passages, and for your tenacity and wit and all the other ways you managed to survive. I am proud of you.

To Mary, for having the courage to give me hope, for guiding me in owning the full story of my life, and for being my therapist of a lifetime.

To Elizabeth Devita-Raeburn, for writing the first book I ever read about sibling loss, for having the courage to share your story, and for speaking directly to my soul.

To Sherry, Farah, Judy, Jill, and other surviving siblings, for trusting me with your story, and knowingly acknowledging mine.

Acknowledgments

To Jamelia, Leah, Reece, Roxanne, and Alysia, for changing the dialogue around grief in the workplace.

To Madeline, for serving as an unfiltered sounding board, and for modeling how to carve out 'me' time.

To Lori R, for nudging me beyond my known zone, and for expanding my realm of probabilities.

To my bosses, colleagues, and mentoring relationships, for broadening my world with your valuable perspectives, and for advocating for me in circles beyond my reach.

To Jhernee', for putting forth my name, and to the Southeast Region of **The WICT Network**, for awarding me the honor of sharing my story with such a large audience.

To Lori T-J, for being the first to encourage me to write a book about my story, and for doing so yourself.

To Mike, for involving me in your songwriting process, and for showing what it takes to dream big.

To Amla and Jules, for sharing your authorship experiences and the lesser-known elements of writing.

To Gwen, for helping me to view writing as my art and to begin owning it.

To Holly Eroh, for your artful eye, and for contributing your stunning artwork for my memoir.

225

To Elizabeth Hill, for being my writing coach and going wherever I needed to go, for being my lead editor and publisher, and for making this long-held dream come true through your team at Green Heart Living

To LaToia, for engaging my heart and mind as a coach, for reviewing my manuscript for inclusive language through Your Big Debut, LLC, and for showing me how to celebrate life.

To my Book Launch Team, for pouring your time, expertise, and energy into extending this message far beyond my scope of influence.

To our Serenberry Team, for freeing me up to focus on my writing by taking care of our customers and grapevines.

To my Inner Trailblazer clients, for choosing to 'go there' with me, and for helping me learn and grow alongside you.

To Yo-Yo Ma, for serenading me with your album, Six Evolutions - Bach: Cello Suites, as I wrote.

To authors, researchers, and publishers, for using your skills, talents, and influence to spark dialogue and deepen our collective understanding about loss, grief, and surviving siblings.

To You, the Reader, for being willing to be vulnerable, for witnessing my core story of loss and grief, and for playing an integral role in spreading the word about *Opening Up to Grief*.

Thank You to every single person who has encouraged and inspired me to be more of who I am meant to be in this world. In big and small ways, you have helped to prepare me for this opportunity: to share my story, so others can know they are not alone.

Resources

Support for Surviving Siblings: Before Adulthood

When I was a teenager, I had posters in my room with concisely clever quotes.

If I were to go back in time and decorate my room for younger me, these are messages I would post:

You are Deeply Loved & Always Will Be.

You are Worthy as You Are.

It's OK to Feel What You Feel.

Your Needs Matter.

The World Needs Your Unique Gifts & Perspectives.

For Young Grievers

For those who have suddenly become a surviving sibling as a child or adolescent, as well as those who are learning to own their sibling loss from years ago, you may find solace in these approaches, or they may spark more ideas.

Ask questions about your sibling.

This can be especially helpful if you are unable to access your own memories. Even with your own recollections, it can be insightful to hear different perspectives.

Here are thought-starter questions for you:

What was my sibling like?

What do you most remember about them?

What do you love about them?

What made them human or less than perfect?

How did we interact with each other?

Express yourself.

Give an outlet for what is in your heart or on your mind through writing in a journal, painting on a canvas, embracing active movement, or another method that feels right for you.

Share your feelings with those who have earned the right to hear your story.

When feeling too stuck or overwhelmed by what is inside, spend quiet time in nature.

Ask for what you need.

Be deliberate in thinking about what you need, and reach out for help.

Realize one person can love you deeply and want what is best for you, yet be unable to meet all of your needs. This does not mean *you* are too much. They may be giving you all they have the capacity to give at this time.

It may be helpful to ask for additional support from another trusted adult.

For Supporters

For those who are a parent, relative, friend, neighbor, teacher, community member, mental health professional - anyone who has influence in the life of a child or adolescent who has become a surviving sibling - you can make a positive and lasting impact.

First of all, thank you for showing up for us.

Losing a loved one is difficult at any age. When it happens before adulthood, we have not yet developed healthy coping skills for grieving. We may have trouble grasping the reality of what happened, and what it means for us.

For this reason, you may find the following actions and activities to be helpful for a young surviving sibling, or they may spark more ideas. Consider your relationship with the surviving sibling to determine what is most appropriate. These are based on my lived experience and learnings from others.

Begin with you.

When you take care of yourself, you are better able to care for the needs of others. Seek support from someone who can help you process your own complex feelings and emotions. This can be a loving friend who is an active and compassionate listener, a grief coach, or a mental health professional.

Imagine yourself in their shoes.

While everyone is different and has different reactions, perspectives, and needs, this can help to tap into the empathy within you. What might it be like to be this child or adolescent who just lost their sibling? How might they feel? What might they need?

Remember everyone grieves differently.

Be attentive to their needs and new behaviors, which may suddenly appear.

Remind them how much they are loved, and show them they are not alone.

Meet the surviving sibling where they are. Hold space for their feelings and emotions, while not pushing them to share. Children and adolescents process grief much differently than adults.

Recognize when they choose a transitional object and honor it. A transitional object may help the surviving sibling feel a sense of security and a symbolic connection with their sibling.

Offer support for grieving.

Find a trusted adult who can relate. This can be a friend or mentor who genuinely understands, is able to listen without judgment, and is willing to exchange stories, feelings, and emotions interwoven with loss and grief.

In addition, it can be beneficial to arrange time with a mental health professional trained to support those who are grieving before adulthood.

Lean on the side of getting external help, as it can be a lifesaver to have an outlet to process difficult emotions without the pressure of considering others' reactions. It also offers a safe environment for learning and developing healthy coping mechanisms, which can serve the surviving sibling for a lifetime.

Send a sympathy card to the surviving sibling.

Receiving a card addressed solely to them can have a long-lasting impact, and will likely be appreciated whenever it arrives.

Elizabeth DeVita-Raeburn, in her book *The Empty Room*, writes about the pattern in the message received by surviving siblings "that the loss is not theirs to mourn."

She continues, "The exception was a handful of people who received a condolence letter addressed solely to them. I was a recipient of such a letter, too. It was written by one of my father's college buddies, who had lost a daughter. Each one of us in this small group still has the letter."

While families may receive a considerable number of sympathy cards in the weeks following their loss, it can be meaningful to send a thoughtful note commemorating a birthday, special occasion, or whenever a kind and heart-warming memory comes to mind.

Help prepare for common questions.

Assure the surviving sibling they will *always* be a sibling, and it is okay to have a different relationship with their sibling than others do.

Let them know, "Do you have any siblings?" is a question people may ask when they are getting to know them, and often have no idea how difficult it can be to respond.

The surviving sibling's age, distance from how long ago their loss occurred, and where they are in the grieving process are all factors to consider when helping them prepare to answer this question. Their response will likely evolve over time.

Use the name of the deceased sibling.

During everyday conversations, include references to the sibling who died. Share stories spotlighting their whole personality - the easy-to-love parts, as well as the human and imperfect parts. This keeps their memory alive, and sends the message they will always be remembered. It is part of the healing process for those left behind.

See additional options under Resources.

Support for Surviving Siblings: In Adulthood

For those who are learning to own a sibling loss from years ago, or from very recently, may you find validation and healing.

Based on my lived experience, and growing collection from being a seeker and finder of caring ways to delve into grief, I offer the following actions and activities for your consideration, and to spark more ideas that speak to your heart.

Be kind to yourself.

Speak to yourself as you would to someone you highly respect and admire. If you become aware of negative self-talk, and find yourself getting steeped in 'shoulds' or a spiral of comparisons, be the friend who sticks up for you.

Recognize there are many layers of grief, and sometimes it may feel like you are revisiting an ache you thought had healed. Remind yourself it is all part of the grieving process.

Give yourself permission to feel your feelings, free of judgment. When you are unable to specifically pinpoint how or why you feel a certain way, remind yourself it is okay. Let the emotions flow through you.

Gaze into the eyes of the one who looks back at you in the mirror, and remind them how loved they are today.

Be mindful of the calendar.

Make a note of significant dates related to your sibling, as well as upcoming milestones you had hoped to share. Birthdays, anniversaries, and other special occasions can be emotional triggers, so it is helpful to be aware of these in advance.

Commit to less than you believe you can manage at the moment. Prioritize the people, places, and activities that bring you supportive energy.

When you need to show up in a certain way, for work or another event, plan mini-breaks or blocks of time to take deep breaths and acknowledge your feelings.

Connect and care for your inner child.

Reflect back on your younger self, the age you were when you first became a surviving sibling. Immerse yourself in doing something you enjoyed at that age, especially if you have not done it a while. Perhaps, it is coloring with crayons, making a mud pie, or riding a bike.

Observe someone who is currently the age you were when your sibling died. Think about how they would experience such a profound loss, and what they might need.

Empathize with younger you. Revisit any difficult feelings or regrets you may have, and extend grace to yourself. To gain a more understanding perspective, consider reading a children's book about grief.

Give yourself what your younger self needs, whether you received it before or not. What would have been comforting to you?

Seek and receive support.

Reach out to someone who will hold space for your loss and grief. Share your feelings, and allow yourself to be seen and acknowledged.

Preserve your energy. Be intentional about with whom you spend your time. Notice how you feel, during or after, interacting with someone. Use your observations to make future decisions.

Use this time to receive support, even if you are more comfortable taking care of others. Jot down tasks needing to be done. When a caring friend says, "let me know if you need anything", ask for their help with a specific task.

Reconnect with your sibling.

Do what feels right to honor your loss - from pausing a few moments and thinking of them to planning a gathering with other loved ones.

Listen to a song they loved. Go to a place they enjoyed, or always wanted to visit.

Sit with an item they relished or a meaningful gift they gave to you. Think about how much joy it brought to them.

Pay attention to your dreams. They tend to be heightened in frequency and intensity after a profound, life-changing loss, and may hold key details of significance. Consider how you felt during the dream, and how it may relate to your grief.

Write a letter expressing what you want them to know. This can be to your sibling at the age of their death or the age they would be today. How do you feel about them? What was left unsaid? In what ways have they influenced your life?

Reflect on your journey.

Check in with yourself and your grieving process. Ask yourself: what's one word to describe how I am feeling right now? This can be a simple way to note how your feelings are changing, even slightly, over time.

Tee up questions to jumpstart your self-awareness and offer essential nourishment. Here are thought-starter questions for you:

How is my grief showing up?

In what ways might I try to bypass my grief?

With the loss of my sibling, what other losses or changes has this led to?

What does 'grieving well' look like for me? What will it feel like?

What do I most need in this moment?

Pay it forward.
Do something to honor your sibling. This can be anything your heart tugs at you to do, whether it is a one time event or an ongoing activity.

Consider your sibling's hobbies, things they enjoyed, or something others in their position may need. The ideas can be endless, such as planting a garden, running a race, or donating blood. Let your intuition lead the way in pursuing what brings the most meaning for you.

Share your story of loss and grief. Honor where you are in the grieving process, and reveal what feels respectful to your journey. This gives others a way to learn more about you and your sibling, and may lead to a deeper connection.

Send a thoughtful note, periodically, to someone who has encountered the loss of a sibling or another devastating loss. Share a resource you found helpful during the grieving process. Encourage them to feel whatever they need to feel, whenever they need to feel it.

Let others know you are still grieving, even after time has passed. By relating your experience, you will help to change the way people look at their own loss and the losses of others.

See additional options under Resources.

Further Support

Organizations

Dougy Center
https://www.dougy.org/
Provides grief support in a safe place where children, teens, young adults, and their families can share their experiences.

Gerard's House
https://gerardshouse.org/about-us/
A safe place for grieving children, teens, and families, where healing happens through acceptance and peer support.

Good Grief
https://good-grief.org/goodgrief/
Builds resilience in children, strengthens families, and empowers communities to grow from loss and adversity.

Kate's Club
https://katesclub.org/
Empowers children and teens facing life after the death of a parent, sibling, or caregiver.

The Compassionate Friends
https://www.compassionatefriends.org/
Supports families after a child dies.

Winston's Wish
https://www.winstonswish.org/
Supports bereaved children, young people, their families and the professionals who support them.

Social Media

Grieving It
www.instagram.com/grievingit

Sibling Grief
www.instagram.com/sibling.grief

Sibling Grief Club
www.instagram.com/siblinggriefclub

Surviving Our Siblings
www.instagram.com/survivingoursiblings

The Grief Space_
www.instagram.com/thegriefspace_

Podcasts

Coming Back: Conversations on Life After Loss
https://shelbyforsythia.com/coming-back-podcast

Grief Out Loud
https://www.dougy.org/news-media/podcasts

Mindfulness and Grief
https://mindfulnessandgrief.com/grief-podcast/

Open to Hope
https://www.opentohope.com/radio/

Surviving Sibling Loss - The Forgotten Mourners
https://podcasts.apple.com/ie/podcast/surviving-siblin
g-loss-the-forgotten-mourners-podcast

Books

Sibling Loss & Grief

Day, Brittany and Eliza. (2021). I'm Still a Big Sister! Brittany Day.

DeVita-Raeburn, Elizabeth. (2004). The Empty Room: Surviving the Loss of a Brother or Sister at Any Age. Scribner.

Donnelly, Katherine Fair. (2015). Recovering from the Loss of a Sibling. Open Road Distribution.

Handler, Jessica. (2015). Invisible Sisters: A Memoir. University of Georgia Press.

Hyatt, DSW., Erica Goldblatt. (2015). Grieving for the Sibling You Lost, a Teen's Guide to Coping with Grief and Finding Meaning After Loss. Instant Help Books.

Mansbach, Adam. (2021). I Had a Brother Once: A Poem, A Memoir. One World.

White, Ph.D., P. Gill. (2008). Sibling Grief: Healing After the Death of a Sister or Brother. iUniverse.

Wolfelt, Ph.D., Alan D. (2008). Healing the Adult Sibling's Grieving Heart: 100 Practical Ideas After Your Brother or Sister Dies. Companion Press.

Loss & Grief Before Adulthood

Hendricks, MS and Nancy Kriseman, LCSW. (2021). We Come Together as One: Helping Families Grieve, Share, and Heal. Kate's Club.

Horsley, Ph.D., MFC, and CNS, Gloria and Heidi Horsley Psy.D., LMSW, MS. (2014). Teen Grief Relief: Parenting with Understanding, Support and Guidance. Rainbow Books, Inc.

Perry, M.D., Ph.D., Bruce D. and Oprah Winfrey. (2021). What Happened to You?: Conversations on Trauma, Resilience, and Healing. Flatiron Books.

Loss & Grief in Adulthood

Dass, Ram and Mirabai Bush. (2018). Walking Each Other Home: Conversations on Loving and Dying. Sounds True.

Forsythia, Shelby. (2019). Permission to Grieve: Creating Grace, Space, & Room to Breathe in the Aftermath of Loss. Shelby Forsythia, LLC. and (2020). Your Grief, Your Way: A Year of Practical Guidance and Comfort After Loss. Zeitgeist.

Okonoa, Nneka M. (2021). Self-Care for Grief: 100 Practices for Healing During Times of Loss. Adams Media.

Zadra, Dan. (2011). In Loving Memory. Compendium, Inc.

Children's Books about Loss

Karst, Patrice. (2018). The Invisible String. Little, Brown Books for Young Readers.

McLeish, Shanice. (2021). Grief on the Playground. Grieving It.

Olivieri, Laura. (2021). Where Are You? A Child's Book about Loss. Lulu.com

Rowland, Joanna. (2017). The Memory Box: A Book About Grief. Sparkhouse Family.

Thomas, Pat. (2001). I Miss You: A First Look at Death. B.E.S.

Bibliography

Auntyflo. (2021). Dream Dictionary, Uncover the truth about your dreams. Auntyflo.

Carroll, Aaron E. (2017). When Children Lose Siblings, They Face an Increased Risk of Death. The Upshot.

DeVita-Raeburn. (2004). The Empty Room, Surviving the Loss of a Brother or Sister at Any Age. Scribner.

Donnelly, Katherine Fair. (1988). Recovering from the Loss of a Sibling. Open Road Media.

Fletcher, Jason & Barbara Wolfe. (2013). A Sibling Death in the Family: Common and Consequential. School of Public Health, Yale University.

Godfrey, Jan-Louise. (2016). Silent grief - the overlooked impact of losing a sibling. Psychlopaedia.

Gunter, Edith Crumb. (2014). Surviving the death of a sibling: a phenomenological study of childhood bereavement. Think IR: The University of Louisville's Institutional Repository.

Kanarek, Lisa. (2021). How 'Transitional Objects' Can Help You Manage Grief. Well+Good.

National Child Traumatic Stress Network Child Traumatic Grief Committee. (2009). Sibling Loss Fact Sheet Sibling Death and Childhood Traumatic Grief: Information for Families. National Center for Child Traumatic Stress.

Okona, Nneka M. (2021). Self-Care for Grief, 100 Practices for Healing During Times of Loss. Adams Media.

Perry, Bruce D., M.D., Ph.D., and Oprah Winfrey. (2021). What Happened to You? Flatiron Books.

Platt, Christine. (2021). The Afrominimalist's Guide to Living with Less. Tiller Press.

Pratt, Elizabeth. (2017). Death of a Brother or Sister Can Shorten the Lives of Surviving Siblings. Healthline.

Romm, Cari. (2016). Little Kids Use Their Dreams to Figure Out Real Life. The Cut.

Shattuck, Lynn. (2020). Instead of the 'Forgotten Mourners,' What if We Called Grieving Brothers or Sisters This Instead? Medium.

Silverman, Phyllis R. and Madelyn Kelly. (2009). A Parent's Guide to Raising Grieving Children, Rebuilding Your Family After the Death of a Loved One. Oxford University Press.

Tawwab, Nedra Glover. (2021). Set Boundaries, Find Peace. TarcherPerigee.

Vanbuskirk, Sarah. (2021). What Does It Mean If My Child Moves Around a Lot While They Sleep? Verywell.

Wade, Breeshia. (2021). Grieving While Black, An Antiracist Take On Oppression and Sorrow. North Atlantic Books.

White, Ph.D., P. Gill. (2008). Sibling Grief, Healing After the Death of a Sister or Brother. iUniverse Star.

Williams, Dr. Chinwé. (2021). How to Help Siblings Cope with the Loss of a Child. Parent Cue.

About
the Cover Art

Holly Eroh is a fine art finger-painting artist. The sunflower on the cover of *Opening Up to Grief* was growing in Downtown Blue Ridge, Georgia. She captured its emotional intensity in oil.

From the artist: "Sunflowers are usually uplifting with their vibrant yellows, oranges and reds, but this particular half open situation made me feel the anticipation of what is yet to come."

IG @ hollymichellefineart

About
Green Heart Living

Green Heart Living's mission is to make the world a more loving and peaceful place, one person at a time. Green Heart Living Press publishes inspirational books and stories of transformation, making the world a more loving and peaceful place, one book at a time.

Whether you have an idea for an inspirational book and want support through the writing process – or your book is already written and you are looking for a publishing path – Green Heart Living can help you get your book out into the world.

You can meet Green Heart authors on the Green Heart Living YouTube channel and the Green Heart Living Podcast.

www.greenheartliving.com

About the Author

Janice Jernigan is an author, guide, and inner trailblazer. Her life's work is deepening connections within, with nature and each other.

Through her lived experience, decades of leading change for one of America's largest privately held companies, and Inner Trailblazer, her business and way of life, she guides those who are willing to 'go there' - into the deepest parts of themselves - in learning, healing, and growing into who they are meant to be in the world.

She and her husband are the founders and cultivators of Serenberry Vineyards in the beautiful mountains near Blue Ridge, Georgia.

www.InnerTrailblazer.com

www.ingramcontent.com/pod-product-compliance
Lightning Source LLC
Chambersburg PA
CBHW070328090426
42733CB00012B/2403